The Bright Streets of Surfside

Isaac Bashevis Singer (left) and Lester Goran, February 1982. Courtesy of Amanda Alcock.

The Bright
~ Streets
of Surfside

The Memoir of
a Friendship with
Isaac Bashevis Singer

Lester Goran

The Kent State University Press
KENT, OHIO, AND LONDON, ENGLAND

PJ
5129
S49
Z69
1994

Library of Congress Catalog Card Number 94-8669
ISBN 0-87338-506-3
Manufactured in the United States of America

Library of Congress Cataloging-in-Publication Data

Goran, Lester.
    The bright streets of surfside : the memoir of a friendship with Isaac
Bashevis Singer / Lester Goran.
        p. cm.
    ISBN 0-87338-506-3
    1.   Singer, Isaac Bashevis, 1904– —Friends and associates.
2.   Goran, Lester. I. Singer, Isaac Bashevis, 1904– . II. Title.
PJ5129.S49Z69 1994
839'.0933—dc20
[B]   94-8669
                                                                            CIP

British Library Cataloging-in-Publication data are available.

~ For Deedee

In memory of our grandson
Daniel Spencer Goran
(October 11, 1985 – October 8, 1989)

～ Bonnie, Bill, and now Britty Goran

Their presence gave us meaning and strength to go on.

 Contents

❧ Acknowledgments

I WOULD LIKE to acknowledge the help and enthusiasm of my two friends Jim Trupin and Gene Clasby in the preparation of this work. Trupin, my agent, was with me every step of the progress toward a manuscript, and Clasby was there—as always—when I needed him.

My special thanks to my sons Bill and John Goran, who witnessed these events over the years and gave me their valuable counsel on things I should have known. I am grateful to my son Bob and his wife, Jill, at whose home in Atlanta parts of the original manuscript were completed. Their understanding and concern for us was a great help in a dark time.

The following people shared with me their memories of Isaac Singer's time at the University of Miami: Peter Townsend, Shaloma Shawmutt-Lessner and Howard Lessner, and Gordon Weel; my former students Stephanie Packer, Mary Webster, Lena Toro, Robert Ratner, Liza Wolman, Emilio San Pedro, Anita Cheng, and Liliana Galdo, as well as Phyllis Shaw and Sister Rita Carey, who were in the last class; Deans Arthur Brown, David Wilson, and Calvin Leonard; my former chairman, Bill Babula, who saw the fun and story in it from the beginning; my present chairman, Zack Bowen; and Mary Hope Anderson.

My thanks to Kathleen Gordon and Arthur Rothenberg, who with every conversation make my decades of teaching seem more purposeful and large.

I learned much about Isaac Singer from two other friends, now gone: John McCollum, who was my counselor for twenty-four years, seven of them in Singer's time; and Richard E. Gerstein, whom I question daily, as if he were still here encouraging and challenging me and, as if it were an easy thing, making the world a better place.

I thank my colleagues John Paul Russo, Robert Casillo, and Peter Schmidt for reading the manuscript at various stages and making a number of useful comments.

A Max Orovitz Summer Fellowship from the University of Miami enabled me to revise the manuscript, and I appreciate this support and encouragement.

Finally, my thanks to Julia Morton and John Hubbell of The Kent State University Press, who treat writing and publishing as callings to be enjoyed and savored.

~ Preface

IN THE TEN years I knew Isaac Bashevis Singer, between April 1978 and about the time he left the University of Miami in 1988, I discovered in him a tendency to exercise his literary skills to remarkable daily effect. He did not merely use his abilities when he formally created his fictions, either alone or when we worked together on his translations. He rewrote all day—and, he assured me, while he dreamed at night—everything around him, people, events, geography, and moral assumptions. Complete in himself, confident of what he understood of narrative, he would correct and revise for people who told him what they thought was a good story. He would pick and choose for me a living person's traits that he wished to embellish as if all that mattered was that he had the final say on whatever, however remotely, touched him.

Surfside, Florida, a community on the northern outskirts of Miami Beach, where he had purchased a condominium several years before I met him, was as familiar to him as the Polish *shtetls* in his imagination. Nothing in the cleaner's shops, restaurants, and bakeries on Harding surprised him. Surfside changed the name of the street leading up to his apartment at 9511 Collins Avenue. It was renamed Isaac Singer Boulevard. He appropriated the waitresses in Shelton Drugs and next door at Danny's Restaurant, and what he did not know by fact he closed off by recourse to his considerable imagination.

We worked together teaching a spring class at the university on Mondays and on Sundays translating his stories from the Yiddish at a small table in the poorly ventilated game room on the first floor of his condominium building.

Proust used to come home from dinners and late at night compose a letter to his host, outlining the events of the evening, the deficiencies and moments of the experience, and then send the letter immediately by coach post so that his recent host would not linger long in doubt about Proust's reaction to the events of the night. The hosts were frequently astonished, perhaps appalled. No one could dispute Proust's facts; they were accurate. It was what he chose to see, what he chose to make of what he'd heard or felt and could commit with his rare eloquence and insight to paper. He reportedly died in bed correcting galleys—little difference, I suggest, from living between the mechanics of writing and the shadowy drama others thought of as real life. I think there is a Marcel Proust in most novelists of sustained commitment, the score-keeping and registration of necessary details, for proportion and comfort, if not Proust's uncanny social and ironical sense of the devilishness in the cruel effect of time on hapless humans.

A searcher after proportion myself, with six published novels when I met Singer, I watched him as closely as I've ever observed anyone except my mother and father. I did not do it consciously, that is to say, in the desire to write a book about Isaac Singer and me. He was peculiar, vulnerable, complex, and active; and I could not keep my writer's eyes away from him.

If I studied him with a sense that he was a man making ripples in the great ponds of history, whether of literature, Jewishness, or some statement toward psychological truth, I was not aware of this element to my scrutiny. He was Isaac Singer to me, personal, tough, a writer: perhaps one gifted beyond any I would know this close but still, here and now, Isaac—with all his vain posturings and majestic abilities. In Hebrew we were both named Yitzchak Silberman, I too on my mother's side. We came from ancestral roots next door to each other in Poland, and it was certainly coincidental that we wound up teaching English 560 together in room 323 of the Ashe Building at the University of Miami, two writers and neighbors with Bilgoray and Bialystok binding and separating us.

Our mutuality meant something to us, but it was only the present air that vibrated, with no historical resonance beyond ourselves. It is probably as intellectually indefensible to overestimate the impact of one's own acts on a historical setting as to ignore the fact that a context might exist. One thinks of the billions of times when some fleeting moment in history, soon to vanish like the bubbles in ocean spray on the beach, began with the self-important announcement "Gentlemen, what we are about to do today..." And then what? After the noble assessments, how, like yesterday, tomorrow became any-how—bubbles on the beach in the vast tides of meaning inherent in historical significance. To paraphrase Dylan Thomas: despite the portentousness of our situation, Singer and I forked no lightning.

My only experience with Isaac Singer's world was the brown-and-white photos of patriarchs in the *Sunday Forward*. When I was a child, in Pittsburgh, I'd cut out these figures with rounded-edge scissors on the floors of the various living rooms where my mother, after reading this paper, would place them. Singer represented to me, if anything personal at all, my mother poring over the Yiddish newspaper, first in easy relaxation, then later wide-eyed behind thick glasses after her cataract operations. Even when she spoke to me of Singer as she read his serials in the *Forward*, I did not connect him to a great Yiddishness or to Judaism. He was her face and her voice, her pleasure in reading and looking at the grand buildings, the animals, the bearded luminaries, and the shawled women that the newspaper featured weekly. She loved Tolstoy in Yiddish and hack writers and Isaac Singer.

I cannot make a metaphor of Isaac Singer anymore than I would dream of making a metaphor of my mother.

One great advantage of reading the world through that nagging writer's eye is to comprehend the chasm between a metaphor, with all its burnished sides turning glibly into meaning from whatever angle it is viewed, and a human being—raw, redundant, contradictory, implausible, foolish, and wise by turns and too swift and necessary to themselves to be anybody's metaphor.

I should have been, for purposes of my narrative, more idealistic to begin with in the book, so that a larger disillusion would then fall on me before my time with Isaac was played out. I should have been braver in rejecting quickly my chores with him—but then there would be no book at all. For a really good story, Singer should not have been pitched so singularly in one driven chord. I should, he should: we were two men moving through our years—he in virtual despair, I without the burdens of destiny and its meaning to me, concerning myself with lost time only in terms of what ordinary people feel.

"Why are you so unhappy?" I asked him once—a frequent question—and he glared at me, not believing that I did not know.

When I shrugged my shoulders to indicate my ignorance, he said, "Old, old, I am unhappy because I am old."

What greater forces could have intruded on me than impending death with its perennially sad tale of watching a brilliant man in the last of winter expiring before the dawn.

Having only the slimmest religious background, I am nevertheless not denied the consolations of religion now when I am old enough to understand the subject; but the absence of an enforced religion in my upbringing saved me from the obsessive quarrel some people—Singer among them—have life-long with the phantoms of the tyranny and superstition they feel were inflicted on them.

Not having a need for a certain sort of drama outside of my own written fictions, I played to no conflict, in a literary and philosophical sense, between Isaac and me. With a limited interest by background and temperament in Isaac's arguments with the Almighty, I felt no call to see myself as an auditor of his battles with his cosmic or earthly adversaries: routinely working with Singer under the extraordinary circumstance cited here in the time we were friends and colleagues, I was not susceptible to the importance success placed on him, the vacillations between arrogance and humility, the mysterious enemies, the conspiracies, and finally what were for me the hollow demands of a faceless future.

A boy cuts out a picture from a Jewish newspaper. His hands are careful not to mar the shape of a Hasid's hat, a rabbi's nose, the tail of donkey standing remotely in a spare meadow.

None is so crazy but that he may find a
crazier comrade who will understand him.

—Heinrich Heine, *Harz Journey* (1824)

~ PART ONE
# Friends

~ Chapter One

IsAAC SINGER and I took a long stroll one morning on a fine spring day, and he seemed to feel particularly good. When this mood was on him he wanted to nod effusively to strangers and agree with everything I said. He usually took me by the arm on such occasions and we walked in Surfside, the city where he lived, north of Miami Beach, like two men one sees at times in 1934 photographs of Prague or Warsaw.

He bent his head to listen as we talked. His attentiveness was a mark of passionate courtesy. He laughed. He looked up into my face.

Were there ever two men more blessed to have found each other? Our delight was sent gamboling out to the bright blues of the day, the sun almost white on the sidewalks. A happy moment was to be allowed us in a world where we two understood darkness: this walk was not a time for what we knew of shadow and pain.

Your father, he said, was after all a man who had been taken advantage of by mercenary and unfeeling people, not a wanderer or a man to be condemned. Your mother was a princess of spiritual kingdoms no one knew except the two of us in our transport of arrival.

I was the greatest friend a man—a poor scribbler like the brother of the great Joshua Singer—ever had. And he was the man most capable of enjoying and understanding the mystical depths of such a friendship.

"You are the ghost of Rachel MacKenzie," Isaac Singer said when we came back to his apartment. He peered up at me through his pale blue-white eyes, waiting for my reaction. "Yes," he said, "yes," in the throes of discovery.

3

I wasn't sure of how a demonologist might mean such a remark. Did he think me inhabited literally or was I being praised to the mystical skies? I knew he had been fond of his late editor at *The New Yorker*.

"That's good," I said vaguely.

"The Almighty sent you," he said. "You were sent by the Almighty."

It was true that he had run through a comparatively dry period before I started "translating" with him, and we had hit with the first ten stories we worked on together; but the Almighty, in truth, unless He had some spectacularly subtle ways He planned to reward my own literary efforts, had not recently caused His blessings to shine on me. I said as much to Singer.

He nodded his head emphatically. "You will win the Nobel Prize too. You will win."

"You see that in my future?"

He held up a copy of his recently published *Collected Stories of Isaac Singer* and said, shaking it at me, "When I was your age I was nothing, I was less than nobody. You will win, my friend."

"My bags aren't packed," I said.

"God sent you," he said fervently. "God sent you. He knew I needed you when Rachel MacKenzie died and He sent you. How can people say He doesn't exist?"

During the spring semester, starting in January, he and I taught together a class in creative writing at the University of Miami. On Sundays I came down to his condominium in Surfside, had breakfast with him, and worked with him on his writing—a process described roughly as "translating." The tags at the end of these stories usually read "Translated by the author and Lester Goran" (or some other name over the years, sometimes Singer's wife, Alma, or other times "translated by the author"). It was actually a clerical refinement of transcription more than a literary exercise. He read to the "translator" in English, putting his Yiddish into a form the auditor could understand, and then the translator put the words down into grammatical or, at best, more idiomatic usage. Singer is not an ornate writer and searches for ways to sound fluent, even slangy; he wanted colloquial-isms or direct slang in the dialogue or the idiomatic in the narration. He was delighted to hear explanations of slang, breaking off our work and almost clapping his hands with pleasure at the derivations of words and phrases.

I then found someone to type the story—on an agreed-upon sum—then edited the typed copy for errors, Xeroxed the material, and had it waiting for him when he arrived at class the next week, or brought it down to him in Surfside midweek if it could be done sooner. He told me to describe myself to people who called him for speaking engagements at the university as his agent, or sometimes he said secretary. My pay in this was to be certain small sums for editing and 10 percent of what the short stories received on publication. He would not hear that I insisted on no money except for a typist. "We will make much money together," he said.

I felt comfortable in his friendship, useful. He seemed so desper-ately to need me: after all, Rachel MacKenzie was gone for good and Isaac was old.

When we left each other on Sundays, after "translating," Singer was often introspective, poured out. Not losing his usual courteous manner on arrivals or departures, though, he shook hands as if one of us were ceremoniously undertaking a break with an old life. He was moody; then he brightened. We would meet again on Monday, but he could not disguise his melancholy.

He needed to recoup and begin a slow process toward recovering himself. He wanted to be away from people to savor what had transpired earlier between us, the jokes and puns, the asides and explanations of Old Poland to a younger admirer. For him it was a heady two-hour session, sometimes three; but the act of sharing his stories as they emerged in English with someone was double-edged. While it had a high exhilaration like a performance act in front of an audience, it had also been a genuine giving away or transformation of a part of himself. He found that, for the moment, debilitating.

Sad, thoughtful, he sought out the forlorn solitude that was his balance to the discomfort he felt in our recent celebrations. I had no sense while he worked that he wrote for posterity or was under any obligation to a set of ideas. Whatever these commitments were, they had been locked in place decades before we met. He wrote to get published, not hiding his opinions, of course, or curbing his impulses, but enjoying the power he had to entertain with his knowledge and obsessions. We edited for publishing words and phrases he found indelicate. Sometimes at my suggestion he pulled back from an antifeminist position, but I made few suggestions of that sort. He had come a long distance without me. His was a brave and bold career, notable for its lack of hesitancy. Strange and calcified, it was what drew me to him. Not a feeling of history unfolding in the orchestrated game room of his condominium, where we worked, but being in the presence of a man seemingly guileless but not afraid of taking chances.

"You are," he told me one day in his unguarded fashion, "the only male friend I've ever had," after revealing some remarkable autobiographical detail of a very strange life. "I never knew men could talk to each other the way we do. I've told women some of these things, they don't understand me anyhow so I can tell them anything. But to tell it to a man is a new thing. This is friendship, yes? This is what it means to have a friend? You are a true friend." He shook his head with wonder. "I heard it all the time. 'I told my friend,' 'I said to my friend'—I didn't understand it—now I know. I am grateful to you, my friend, in ways I cannot tell you."

He touched in me a sense of my mother's unaffected candor. She had loved his work in Yiddish. The decades since then seemed shrouded in deceptions when I observed the easy simplicity of his charm. Life *was* kinder then: the people back then were more easily read and he brought all that back. Perhaps not only to me. It was not an intellectual matter.

Ingmar Bergman—Singer described the scene to me—had leaned forward, recognizing the power and the artless control, at a luncheon in Sweden and kissed Singer's hand and said, "You are the master of us all."

. . .

Singer had come to speak before a Jewish group at the Hillel House at the University of Miami in April 1978, six months before he was awarded the Nobel Prize for literature. When Bill Babula, the chairman of English, and I asked him to teach a course with us, he had only one condition: that it be a course in writing, not one having anything to do with Jewish studies.

For one class a week one semester a year—which he would teach with me, each of us discussing students' stories alternately—he would receive $30,000. Broken down into an hourly rate—three hours on Monday afternoons, counting the hours traveled from his home in Surfside and back—it came to about a thousand dollars an hour. Every semester for our ten years together, Singer found some pressing business in New York he had to attend to in April, leaving every year two to three weeks early—raising his salary average considerably.

"Who's the boss?" he asked me halfway through the first semester.

"No one cares if you miss two weeks," I said.

"But who is it will know to fire me?" he asked.

"Me."

"You won't tell?"

"I promise."

From the start we faced a basic problem in class. He wanted to answer questions with the sweeping authority and privileges of a celebrity come to call, accepted even when vaporing.

Students and I too were to be involved in a conspiracy of sorts. Our students were anxious for Singer's anarchy at first, some of them, but after three or four weeks awe dissipated. Singer became an uncertain man from another generation, at a considerable distance from their concerns.

He never retreated from the role of visiting dignitary.

Pushed with questions too specific, opinions too firmly held, or impatient student manners, he bridled like a thoroughbred before the prospect of a fire engine. Mostly he strove for the whimsical tone, insisting to the eventual shuffling of feet (in one horrendous class hisses) and clearing of throats that "There are no rules."

Singer was, unless he turned giddy for various reasons, an austere man. He presented to students and authority a front of sobriety and personal rigidity. Some students in imaginative writing seek rules like the religious seek natural law. They assembled purposefully to learn the art and process behind the royal road to success, a secret, one of the seven well-articulated keys in a how-to-make-a-million scheme.

Many suspected there was a formula for doing it right, to be revealed to them by this ill-matched pair. Others assumed that their teachers to this point were too dumb to have learned the formula. But surely a Nobel Prize winner knew.

Isaac Bashevis Singer had for me one large answer to student inanities. He told me early, "Writing is playful. A game, you understand? It's all play, writing. Like children, a great writer is a child." I mostly agreed. Theoretically, we were at no great distance from each other. Then he added, "But don't tell the students."

Their worst nightmare: the seventh key known but kept secret from them.

"What difference would it make?"

"We'll be fired."

"Isaac!"

"No, no, my friend, no kidding around. Be serious."

Inexorably, it dawned on each class: Isaac Bashevis Singer was judging their work by the *subjects* they wrote about.

He carried about a meaning in himself. He sat in a seersucker jacket, narrow-shouldered, yellow-toothed, and blinking as if he too was astonished to find himself a transatlantic Rip van Winkle three generations late in America. Torn whole from my imagination and complete with Yiddish inflection, and gesture of the *shtetl* and pre-1935 Warsaw, he confronted our students and modernity with rage and eloquence and a ready story or anecdote to rebuke "the professors."

Surely there were young men in that long-vanished Poland. But from the minds of descendants from those places, like me, there had vanished the bare-armed farm boys and Yeshiva youths (except in the pale flesh of tragic pictures taken hours before their ghastly deaths), and we deal now only in the collective vision of the past with the *zehde*, the grandfather, a grandmother, Isaac Singer in the flesh.

Archaic, unworldly, sanctified by age and European disasters, Isaac Singer came to us all intact and preserved, a figure we all knew. Learning how to write was an artifice beneath him, an American softness. He was accorded the virtues of kindness and generosity, or else we denied our lineage and its worth.

To his credit, he knew what had been bestowed on him. He knew that he represented an old order ordained to righteousness and he could use it for advantage and he could trade on it, but only so far. And he knew that trifling with his status, the role, could devour him and make of his lifelong efforts to be an important writer an asterisk to the unbearable rolling decades of horror.

He never strayed far from doom. He assured a woman student that the father and daughter in her story running away with a racehorse from a tyrannical wife and mother could only commit incest to make her story good. The class was unsure. They looked down at their notebooks.

The student asked me after class, "Should I change that in the story? It's not what I had in mind. Honest, its about my father and me."

When in *Enemies* Masha's mother laments that her landlord is worse than the Nazis, the reader might be puzzled by Singer's lack of control in not censoring his characters in the name of believability. But around him, his passion—even in withdrawal, as charged as a slumbering lizard waiting for a hapless housefly—he drew emotional turbulence.

From my introduction to him on, people around him stepped forward, took position downstage left, and announced their darknesses, pains, and resolutions.

The first week he came to class with his wife, Alma, and another woman I'll call Ursula. Classes were in motions of students and people coming to see him, perched on chairs, departing in midsentences, sitting on the floor. Singer was clever and tart; he, and everyone else, was pleased with his performance. When we went to the cafeteria, he stopped Babula when Bill went to pick up the tab for the coffee. "Let them pay," he said, indicating Ursula and Alma. He made a scornful face. "Don't spend a penny on them."

Men together, he said he was reminded of the Warsaw Writer's Club when he spoke to Bill and me (considering the host of failures, eccentrics, and poseurs I later learned were there, not the compliment I first heard it to be).

Ursula was the wife of a wealthy Latin American. She was traveling alone in the United States. She had specifically come to Miami to study with Singer. Not yet enrolled, she took me aside after three sessions and said this wasn't what she expected. Singer could not help her. "He is not a teacher," she said. I assured her she could learn from Singer.

"Do you have women like Ursula in mind when you write?" I asked.

"Yes, absolutely. Of course, what else?"

"Do you think she's attractive?"

"All right," he said. "Not a beauty. All right. But crazy like the rest of them."

Ursula called me at my office the following week and said she had plenty of money and wanted to study with me.

"Study what?" I asked. "I teach contemporary lit, the eighteenth-century novel, a course in fiction writing."

"I have a manuscript. I'll pay you," she said. "I'll give you whatever you want. I have money."

Singer was often struck the longer we knew each other by how different my life—an American life, Jewish still, and therefore comprehensible by divine right to him—should be so unlike anything he could imagine. I was a trial to him both as a person and as an artist.

"Tell me," he asked. "Women come to you? When you were with women, they come to you?"

"No," I said, "never."

"Never? Women never come to you?"

Mostly what I knew about life, or what had been my experiences, he treated like stale old news. My family, my friends, the cities of the north, the students at the university—"It has happened to many men," he said to me, often, in dismissal.

He blurted out, "I've never had a woman who didn't come to me. Never, in all my life. If she doesn't come to me nothing happens. I would not know how to seduce a woman."

"Surely," I said, "with all the many women you've had you pursued some."

He sat looking down at the table in Danny's, in Surfside, and I realized he intended to tell me something honest. He was tapping his finger as he mentally counted.

"Thirty," he finally said, "and they all came to me." He looked at me expectantly. "That's a lot of women?"

"Plenty," I said.

"Really, a lot?"

"Well, figure one a year, that's thirty years' worth of women."

"And you, my friend, now you must tell me how many women you've had in your life."

"Less than a thousand."

He laughed, reddening. "Please, tell me," he said.

"Not as many as you," I said.

"Ah," he said, "see, you're honest, that's why I admire you."

Ursula called me at home the following weekend. "You must visit me tonight," she said.

Demons would dance on I-95 and her room would be set afire by supernatural agencies. I'd greet a man there who would look like my long-dead father. Ursula would turn out to be The Evil One in disguise.

"No," I said quickly. "It's a terrible night out."

"I will give you anything you want," she said. "I must go home on Monday and we must work together. God allowed me to find you. I'm not a bad person. I've committed no crime. If God took the veil away from my eyes about Isaac Singer he let me discover you."

"Ursula," I said, "this is foolishness."

"I'll give you two thousand dollars if you come tonight. I have the check here, for you."

Was it really drops of rain on the windowpane and not the gentle rapping of demons?

"No, it's impossible."

That was in 1979, and I have not heard from her since that night. But it was an adequate preparation for the cosmos of Isaac Singer where he told me women have sex with men for only three reasons: they are in love, they are nymphomaniacs, or they want money.

I asked, "How about boredom?"

"I never heard such a thing in my life," he said.

Thus, we had a great many problems with the sex in the stories written by women in our classes. "They are *all* whores!" he exclaimed angrily after class one day, sex in that semester's stories being not explained by love or psychopathology or prostitution but merely something else young people do in student stories.

As a man with profound insights into character, as his fiction attests, Singer often used his gifts to invent plots in life that were not there. When he said in "The Son" that "each face gave its secrets and I seemed to know how each of their brains was working," he qualified it with, "Perhaps I imagined it . . ." but there were no such hesitations outside his fiction.

He would make the world conform to his vision of it if it did not. Speaking casually to me one day after class in our first semester, he asked, "You have sex with the women in class?"

"Not one woman."

I had been married for twenty-six years at the time and had three sons, one or the other of whom attended the university during that time. "I think I have a reputation as a holy-joe."

"Don't tell me," he said, narrowing his eyes. "You sleep with half the women in our class."

"Do you really believe that?" His mind as a writer was an fascinating as his ordinary perceptions were strange and unlikely; but I could track his fancy here.

"Yes, I know it to be the case," he said.

"What gives you your clues?"

"You say hard things to them in class and the women still like you."
"I tell them the truth as I understand it about their work," I said.
I had been teaching writing for twenty years before he came.

"Who are those women you meet in the corridors?" he asked,
clinching the argument. He believed his unerring vision had caught
events and characters other people had missed, things concealed.

"It's between classes when we have a break," I said. "Those are
students walking outside between classes. I know them, I say hello to
them."

"Listen," he said, "I know what I see. Bring some of those women
you talk to out in the corridor into the classroom. You leave the good
ones out there. The ones out there are the ones I want to see. These!"
He dismissed our female students with a wave of his hand and laughed
heartily and touched my arm. "You don't fool me, my friend," he said,
looking at my surprise and reading it for awe, believing himself a
mystical conduit through which truth came to readers. Hadn't he
once presciently fled Poland before the world fell apart?

Walking with me one sunny day among the artfully gardened and
tastefully shaded expensive stores of the Bal Harbour Shops, a mall
several blocks from his condominium, Singer turned to me without
preliminary and said, "You are a natural aristocrat, my friend."

"A poor boy," I said. "That's all, covering it up."

"No, I see it in your face," he said. "You have your mother's face.
She was an aristocrat too: you are both noble people. It's a thing from
nature, aristocracy, it's not from money or a wealthy background. You
are a noble man and your mother was noble before you."

I could not bring myself to disagree with one of the great appraisers
of human character in our time. But he was often in his intuitive
judgments demonstrably wrong.

During our translating sessions I sometimes crept away in my mind
into my own past while doing the mechanical job of turning Isaac's
occasionally broken English into serviceable idiom. My wool-gathering
could include a recent lunch or a conversation held twenty years
earlier, neither exalted nor melancholy, merely there, triggered by

something Singer was saying or by my own interior monologue started in dreams the night before. He stopped, leaned across the table to look directly into my face, or sat back in pleasure. "Huh?" he asked. "You liked that? You like the story? We are doing good, right? This story is very good, I can see it in your eyes, your face. You cannot hide your pleasure."

I turned back to the table from a rancorous vision of a boy who had cheated me at marbles in an alley behind our house when I was twelve. "It's brilliant, Isaac," I said.

"You see," he said, "I can tell. Your eyes were laughing. You could not contain yourself."

I wanted my marbles back then and I do today.

When he told me another time that I was a natural aristocrat, I asked, "How can you tell? I seem a negligent man to myself."

"In your face, your eyes. Who is to say a natural aristocrat shouldn't be negligent?"

"Then it's a physical thing."

"No, you are of a fine moral character too."

"God help the human race," I said.

"The human race, my friend," he said, "is 90 percent brutes and fools, absolutely. Don't you know that?"

"Ninety percent?"

"Absolutely."

"If there are so many brutes and fools, how can someone who isn't a brute or a fool tell someone like himself from the brutes and fools?"

"You and I know each other," he said. "The rest know too."

He shrugged his shoulders to close the conversation. "They find each other. We know, we know."

About two years later I asked him, "You told me a while ago the human race is composed of 90 percent brutes and fools. Have you changed your mind?"

"Yes," he said. "Ninety-*seven* percent brutes and fools. I was too generous."

The cramped seating arrangements in our early classrooms at the University of Miami led to some startling juxtapositions (1982). Courtesy of M. L. Carlebach.

Up close he could not read me—or others—any better in our classrooms. Physically, we were arranged with Isaac sitting at a table at the head of the class while students sat in chairs facing him or in our small conference room on the third floor of the Ashe Building on the campus at the University of Miami. He sat at a large table with the class. I sat in the lecture rooms off to one side, perhaps six feet away on a chair against the wall (or in the early days, when our classes were large, about twenty, I lolled on a radiator one semester). A student sat with him at the table and read aloud his or her story. Singer sat listening, in apparent rapt attention.

As the students read the stories, it became apparent that Singer had not only not read the stories I asked the students to turn in a week early, but he wasn't listening when they read them.

"This happened in Harlem?" he asked a black student who had knowingly planted palm trees all over her story and hibiscus bushes too to indicate Jamaica.

"He was a man who was her uncle?" he asked another student.

"No," the student said, "there isn't an uncle in the story."

"Yes, go on please," Singer said.

At first I put us into a large classroom to accommodate the numbers of people who wanted to see him; but he couldn't see the front row. He insisted on calling on students when he heard a motion. His calls were often into vacancy, where students turned to look when no one had raised their hands. While a student (or I) spoke, Singer abruptly said, "Anyone else, please," not hearing the first student or me.

Year after year students shouted their stories into his inattention. He sat in quietly somnolent reveries, rocking, eating a piece of a cookie, eyes partially closed or shuffling through his coat to discover some remembered paper in an inside pocket.

"Go on, go on," he said as the student stopped and he frisked himself repeatedly.

When we distributed copies to everyone in the class he still insisted, after seven years, that the students read their words louder. Exasperated, a student finally asked, "Why do I have to read louder? Everyone has a Xerox copy of my story in front of them."

Bewildered, Singer said, "You must read louder for yourself."

When Singer said, "Roots," to students, "write from your roots," I think he meant, vaguely, be loyal to what you were, do not make a pretense of being anything else. He was, if I understood him, quarreling with his brother, Joshua, I. J. Singer, who had chosen to write in Polish while Isaac wrote in Yiddish. Polish had seemed, at one time, to Isaac a shabby affectation of the assimilationist; but what Isaac Singer was heard to say to an American audience was something else. They heard him to mean they should find their ethnic—or religious—background and write about that, if not out of that experience. He told one student, born in Miami and revealing no particular ethnic or religious background in his story, to make the two characters in the story "immigrants."

The student, and the class, but not I, was bewildered and passed it off as a joke, but Isaac was not fooling. The devious characters in the student's story, with their pettiness and spying on each other, could be only in his mind, presumably, Polish immigrants, probably Jewish immigrants if they were to be real in America at all.

Under scrutiny, he maintained a stiffness in his posture, painful to observe. Relaxed, he fell into red-faced quips and unintentional revelations of his state of mind. He lost the thread altogether, turning inward frequently and then returning with a non sequitur. "You know, my young friend," he said once, "you would not talk that way if you were born in Poland." The student nodded.

Isaac Singer returned to that ghostly land where everything was discernible to him from long association physically and in his thoughts. He had spent such great energy surviving his years in Europe that he had little will or need to think about America. He made daily, even minute-by-minute, instantaneous translations from the present American to the old Polish landscape. "She would not have dressed like that in Poland," he said, after a conversation with one young woman—she at the feet of the Prophet, he thinking her lipstick made her look like a prostitute.

"Not much chance," I said. "She's Irish."

"Ah," he said, "she's Irish." He smiled gently. It did not matter. He had placed her in a restaurant in Warsaw or on a hillside near Bilgoray. For him that was enough. He was not as much comfortable with the young woman—she was gone, another shadow on our campus—but the thought of her and his old times she had recently renewed. He smiled at the movements, the manner of the young woman in his mind. Far away and Polish.

It made contemporary Coral Gables bearable.

He said frequently, "Write what you know about," insistently, with a persistency that held a desperation to it as annual credo. He also said emphatically every semester, "The only rule, students, is that there are no rules," voicing a conviction born of unfamiliarity with that particular literary minihomily.

When someone asked, "How can anyone write fantasy or historical novels out of what they know about?" he first became sanguine and said, "It can be done, it can be done." Then he became angry and withdrawn.

"Can a woman write out of a man's roots." he was asked, and, turning to me, he asked me to repeat the question and then retreated. "A good writer can write like a man or woman. Only stay with your own address."

The "roots" doctrine lay deeply buried in a quarrel between two Polish-Jewish brothers. The metaphor strangled our Monday afternoons.

I said to him one Sunday, "Isaac, I'd like to talk to you about telling these kids to write about their roots. These students come from divorced homes; some have lived in five cities, ten cities. At this minute they're living in dormitories with other students, and when they're adults they'll look back on this time as the most important in their lives. This might be roots to them. They have programs, whole weekends, at colleges called 'homecomings,' and a lot of the people who return for these college celebrations think of our university as another home. Do you see? These are their roots, what you see right now. They have limited religious backgrounds. They don't know if they're Dutch or German or Huguenot. It's too bad, but that's the way they are."

He looked at me sadly. "You can't be a writer without roots."

"Having a mother who's been divorced three times has to be their roots; there's nothing else for them. They are what they are."

"They're not writers," he said. "It's impossible to be a writer without roots."

"Then if they can't be writers before they even try, what are we doing?" I asked.

"We're taking money," he said, "how you say, under false pretenses." He laughed heartily. "Right, my friend?" he asked. "We're swindlers."

I laughed wearily. He was part right.

The question of the teaching of writing as a failing quest is of course naively based on a belief that there is some absolute standard or model to which the student writer should aspire. If the student was expected to learn how to write like Thomas Mann, then our situation was indeed hopeless; but if we taught the student to improve himself or herself according to their own dispositions, we were doing our jobs. But their dispositions should be allowed to vary. As many times as I tried to reason with Singer about Henry James's conception of fiction as being a house of many reflecting windows, each window not taking precedence over any other window, I don't think he could believe it even though he agreed.

Conversations with Singer were often difficult. We could talk easily about old Poland and escapades with women. But generally other people presented him with distinct, sometimes never-to-be-mentioned-again problems. Edmund Wilson, a favorite of mine, had nominated Singer for the Nobel Prize, but Isaac mistrusted him.

He loathed Barbra Streisand. He said that in his condominium she had tried to lecture him on Jewish cooking and that she had falsified shtetl life in her movie of his short story "Yentl."

He did like Charles McGrath at The New Yorker and Mr. Shawn (he said they were prophets), but little else.

He said William Styron had no business writing about the Holocaust. (A gentile, he could have no feeling for the subject.) He said his sworn antagonist was Elie Wiesel. He claimed that Wiesel had said to a friend of his in Paris, "Isaac Singer is the worst enemy the Jews have after Hitler."

He told me that his early champion, Irving Howe, another favorite of mine, knew little about Judaism and no more about him. He said that Saul Bellow was a writer who made no sense. "What does 'A Foot in His Mouth' [an abridgment of a Bellow title] mean?" he asked. He shook his head negatively as I tried to explain.

He could not sit through movies. He never listened to music. He walked past paintings with the air of a man being insulted.

Paul Kresh, who had written a biography of Singer, he described as a *schmearer*, a flatterer. Kresh was never to be mentioned favorably. Singer's manner was to jockey for advantage with the more appealing of the options available to him. If there were two people besides himself he deftly indicated annoyance with one and courted the other.

During our first meeting, he pulled Bill Babula aside in the university cafeteria and whispered, "Don't pay for them. Let them pay for themselves." He meant to exclude his wife, Alma, and the woman visiting with them at the university. He had become Bill's friend in a conspiracy: he was protecting him from the loss of the dollar their coffee would cost. The women did not expect Babula to pay for their coffee. Still, his manner insinuated that Bill, a stranger, was about to be victimized but for his timely intervention.

He loved the chicanery of the moment's *kunz*, or trick.

Singer's stories, as we worked on them, particularly their language, were real to him, but often a joke on someone or something. We would, between the two of us, take a word or a phrase from a story we had shared and give it a secret—frequently highly private, if ambiguous—meaning. We took the line "Let's not scatter our forces" that a foolish, Left-wing woman says in "The Interview" and repeated it to each other for years. It always made him laugh to hear it. I would say it to him when he departed class sometimes. It cheered him to hear the line. The woman who says it in the story has a few forces either to scatter or retain. It was an ironic comment on a powerless optimism.

Singer invited me to a University of Miami social function to which whoever did the inviting had not chosen or had forgotten to include me on the A List. It was made up of many representative authorities—few, if any, faculty. He insisted I accompany him and his secretary, Devorah Menashe, who was in town for a few days. I agreed, after some urging: these are not necessarily places or events someone choosing spontaneity and the richness of life would choose to go first. Voluntarily, I do not usually go all on my own even when invited. I need no disinviting to persuade me to stay home. But I went.

"You will be my guest," he said happily, the mischief of the occasion seducing his usual, pristine sense of social form.

I do not think anyone in great urgency did not want me present. The then head of the FBI, William Webster, was there; Isaac Bashevis Singer, too; and I sat with a friend in the administration I had known for years. We talked as easily as we had for decades. I was not, my point is, served overcooked fish or ground glass in my salad.

I sat talking with the other people at my table when I was aware of a sort of stillness. Singer, his secretary behind him, had left the podium and slowly was walking across the large room. I turned to look. He seemed very sober. And deliberate. He did not turn to observe the people looking up at him as he passed. He walked in a measured pace around tables and chairs, slowly because there were pitfalls to trip him on all sides. I had never before seen him attempt to negotiate himself into awkward places; usually he was cautious about his footing and eyesight.

He advanced on me. He put his hand around my neck and whispered in my ear, "Let's not scatter our forces."

He spoke fervently to me in private about our students after class, calling them whores, spoiled, stupid, insane, or criminal. He misapprehended details in their fiction to make his own fiction about them. In class, though, he described me—with a slight smile—as vicious or paranoid or nit-picking, a series of categories highly acceptable to a student who has just had a story criticized. About Alma he gave me sinister weekly reports. (She would tell me her version of events when she caught me alone.)

Courting his audience, he presented God, in his remarkable repertory of books, with a subpoena outlining various charges against Him: a tool of the Nazis, an indifferent taskmaster, a capricious architect. With his considerable gifts, he made his readers co-conspirators. Now there is only to understand what conspiracy he had forced on God to court Him, and that I cannot answer.

Serious conversations with Singer, unless they were in certain well-trod territory, were exercises in good listening.

Exasperated, a week after Singer brushed off something I said as "Technical, technical, these people did not come here to hear your technicals," I asked him in class, "Why did they come here?"

"To learn to be writers," he said.

"And what will we teach them?"

"To be true to their roots."

"I don't know how to do that," I said. "Could you explain?"

"Yes," he said, shouting. "Look into their eyes, they are all writers. I see sincerity in their eyes, I see good people. These people will all one day be writers."

Later, walking to his ride, he said to me *sotto voce,* "It's good when we argue. They learn."

~ Chapter Two

SINGER TOLD ME, and others, that he had lied in all his writings—not just in the fiction, where one would expect alterations of fact, but in his autobiographies. He told me that he had omitted certain things relevant to his philosophies and that certain facts about himself had never been made known. I wasn't sure if this was true: interviews with him and autobiographies were instruments that Singer used to identify himself—often apparently to himself, too.

He explained to classes with pleasure, when I asked him questions, "This man never runs out of questions." He laughed. "Ask, ask, Professor, I'll answer."

Outside of class, our conversations often fell into an interview format. He answered, sometimes according to a program in his mind that repeated oft-recited verities, other times in variations on familiar themes; on rare occasions, intense and direct, he said he had never told anyone this and then set forth a revelation (frequently it, too, a twice-told tale). Recognizing his joy and need to recreate himself, in a sort of secular fashion writing while not putting words down on paper, I asked away to my heart's content. But he wanted more. He wanted me from the start to do a biography of him.

We were to be united eternally on a question-and-answer honeymoon. It was, from his point of view, security against not being a writer or feeling like one. A sort of edge or high between the excitements of conception, writing, and publication. As long as the questions and interest continued, he would be aloft and safe. Undiscovered except as he willed it.

He gloried in being questioned, quipping and outrageous, sad and exalted. He said, rapt, "We'll have some fun this afternoon"—meaning, "We'll sit somewhere and you'll ask questions and I'll answer."

23

By the twentieth or so request to write his biography, he became desperate at my lack of interest. "I'll tell you things I never told anyone," he said. "Great things."

Equally desperate, I said, "I'm your friend, not your biographer."

Singer, from his Polish days, liked trashy apparitions with the same enthusiasm he embraced Talmudic paradoxes, ghost stories, two-headed babies, and wise-cracking demons behind the looking glass. In his mind, side by side with these uncritical exposures to the supernatural, lay complex ironies and mysteries of the sciences. He liked astronomy—when it was poetically paradoxical.

We rushed after class sometimes up to South Miami where I bought him a *New York Times* so he could, sitting in the car, check the day's science column, reading about the latest from a Jupiter probe. He was like a gambler with the morning line at Gulfstream. He chuckled at the paper; he agreed with what came back from Jupiter.

He followed rigorously diets limiting cholesterol and animal fats. He did not eat egg yolks and never touched alcohol, but he ate egg-salad sandwiches and raisin pudding. He was a well-known vegetarian. He walked to a wristwatch, counting seconds. It was a system. (He also listed fanatically in a small notebook the names of future characters in vocational, class, or educational categories. He matched up the names of his characters with events.) When he could not walk on Collins Avenue he paced the ninth-floor corridor in his condominium building like a prisoner with twelve minutes of yard time, checking his watch frequently. He told me he methodically paced in his apartment too.

He could in all gravity insist that he had seen in the eyes of farm animals, cattle particularly, an awareness that they are going to die cruelly; in the eyes of certain people nobility; in my own eyes amusement—mistakenly. He resorted to quackery, telling students that he could see in their eyes that they had the capacity to write fiction. However misleading it was to Isaac himself, whether in fakery or sincere belief, that he could read souls through the eyes, it certainly formed craters in the landscape of his fiction when he let this particular nineteenth-century convention take charge as he did in his novel *The Penitent*.

In the 1983 Farrar, Straus and Giroux edition of *The Penitent*, he has his central character say, " 'I saw in their eyes something I had never seen among modern Jews: love for Jewishness, love for a fellow Jew, even if he was a sinner.' " He also writes, "Her eyes reflected the goodness of the true Jewish mother, not the mothers mocked in goodness of the true Jewish mother, not the mothers mocked in books and plays, and whom American Jewish writers and some psychoanalysts consider the source of their children's nervous afflictions." And he closes with the hot breath of prophecy: "Secondly, I saw that she glowed with the grace of chastity. The concept that the eyes are the windows of the soul is not a mere figure of speech. You can see in a person's eyes whether he is full of arrogance or modesty, honesty or cunning, pride or humility, fear of God or abandon. This young woman's eyes reflected all that is good about the Jew. Her gaze revealed all the great qualities mentioned in the *Path of the Righteous*. When she saw me, a stranger, she took a step backwards."

When he did not face people or events in a Polish landscape he bestowed Jewishness upon them. It was not extraordinary. Most of the associations that touched him all his life *were* Jewish. He insisted that our dean was Jewish, our chairman, Bill Babula, and the man who followed him in that position. None of them were.

He listened to my explanations of the life and work of our second chairman, John Paul Russo, an Italian American with a Roman Catholic background, and he said, patiently, "He's Jewish." I explained his education, his family, his place of birth and his writing.

He smiled to himself at my naiveté.

"Jewish, Jewish," he said. "He's Jewish, like you, like me."

"You're right," I said, "he's Jewish. He's hiding."

"See, you know I'm right."

About women, Singer also received divine intimations.

Simon Weber, Singer's friend and editor at the *Forward*, is quoted in Paul Kresh's *The Magician of West 86th Street* as saying that Singer told him that Alma had been trained for a thousand years in the German fashion to be a wife and that he would do nothing to disrupt the process. Taken lightly, it is Isaac Singer looking for the bright aside: examined closer, his relations even with Alma, his wife of decades, were colored by certain—bizarre—literary conceits. While he never told me the exact thing he told Weber, he did tell me that one must outshout a wife, greet her for weeks after an argument with angry silence, and, if necessary, strike her, to show her her subservient place. Being married to him, even for a woman with the formidable qualities of love for him that Alma had, was not easy. She battled a lifetime of belief in Isaac, an adherence to the confused philosophies of his youth.

I visited the Singers for ten years, often in all manner of circumstances—sickness, harmony, rage, and health. There was kindness vying with pettishness in Alma, pragmatism contending with the girlish manner she retained in her eighties. But where Isaac was concerned there was a predatory indifference about her. Everyone was the enemy.

The daughter of a Frankfurt retail merchant—well-to-do, upper-middle-class, as she described her comfortable home in Germany— she said she attended school with Thomas Mann's daughter. She was acutely aware of social distinctions and proprieties. Yet as a married woman at the time, she had succumbed to the admittedly limited charms of Isaac Singer, threadbare, shy to silence, the model of an escapee from a Polish yeshiva.

As he explained to me, within Alma's hearing, just before their memorable meeting he had been reading the work of Otto Weininger, a violent antifemale writer of the early twentieth century. "I still believe what he said," Isaac said, as sitting across from us Alma waved a hand at him in dismissal. "Man is the master," Singer said, quite seriously. "Women are incapable of anything except childlike tasks. No woman can lead, no woman can do anything but raise children: they are too emotional. I have not seen one thing in my life to change my opinion."

"Dooly!" Alma said, using a pet name. "Lester's going to take you seriously."

"My dear woman," he said, "my friend knows my opinions. He knows I'm not joking."

"Isn't he terrible?" Alma asked.

"He is," I said. "But he's serious."

Her face became sad. She looked old and remote suddenly. "I know," she said, "he's serious."

Isaac nodded vigorously.

"I met him in the Catskills," Alma said. "He came to the boarding house where I was staying."

"I was escaping from Hungarians," Singer said. "I never saw such food, *trefe* [nonkosher]. I was among gentiles and the food was going to kill me. Where she was staying the food wasn't good, but it was Jewish anyhow."

"Isaac, it was Jewish food," she said. "You just didn't like it."

"Hungarians," he said with a snort.

"He was very handsome," Alma said, "shy, red hair and with wonderful manners. He looked so lost."

Isaac glanced down shyly. "I couldn't get a word in edgewise with all the female chatter there," he said.

"Dooly, you were polite," she said. "You always are."

"Next year I'll become aggressive and win two Nobel prizes," he said.

"Was it love at first sight?" I asked.

"Oh, what a questioner you are!" she said. "Why do you want to know that?"

"Maybe I'll write about you and not mention Isaac," I said.

"No one would read it," Isaac said, "not a book about her. Not a book about me." He covered fast.

"Well, was it love at first sight?" I asked.

"Yes, you might say so," she said.

She went on to describe him at the kosher table in the Catskills, their walks together, his fund of reading. He read to her; he talked about books and authors. He could not stop talking about Otto Weininger.

When she excused herself from her reveries after a while and went across the room to see a friend, a certain Sally who generally materialized across rooms or streets filled with traffic in Surfside on Sundays, Isaac's face became red with what could have been suppressed laughter. His eyes watered.

"I thought to myself when I saw her the first time," he said, "Oh God, thank you for not cursing me with such a woman. Who could have committed a curse terrible enough to have such a woman visited on him? Everywhere I looked she was there. Who could handle such a woman? Who can handle any of them? But this one: I thanked God I had no connection with her."

"Alma was beautiful," I said. "I've seen pictures of her."

"Who needs any of them?" he asked.

When Alma returned, I asked her, "What was a romance like in those days?"

"Ah," she said, deciding to give me the feel of the time, if not the details, "the adventures we had, the places we'd meet. It was a very confined time and I was unhappy and Isaac was no help."

When I asked him later that day as we walked along the gilt and lights of the Bal Harbour shopping center, "Is it a secret or a mystery? Was it terrible when she left her children?"

He shook his head. "We met in places where people meet. Where should we meet? I didn't know what I was doing. Women are wild. I didn't want to marry. What man wants to marry? Marriage is arranged for the benefit of women and children. It's not for a man."

"You've been together a long time."

"A habit."

How devious Singer's bookish path when he expounded for Alma on those bright Catskills days the philosophy of the half-mad writer from Vienna, Weininger, whose name has become a synonym for the cracked, harebrained, and howling. When talked about at all Weininger is the cultural straw in the wind for the voice of the antifeminist and "Anti-Semite" (his typography) in the dreadful time at the beginning of the century when the cacophony of free and searching voices narrowed down to Hitler's.

Weininger was Jewish. He insisted he was against neither women nor Jews, but he held the theory that women were innately inferior to men and that a fault of Jews (and he said there was this Jewishness in most people, except those who were Aryan) was an excess of the feminine in their nature. In a series of paradoxes he said that all the great men who were anti-Semitic (like Goethe or Wagner) had a certain Jewishness in their nature and this allowed them to confront the hateful stain in other people.

Weininger published his one book in 1903 (the edition I read of *Sex and Character* was from 1906, a sixth printing) and he committed suicide at age twenty-three that same year. His book has the looney order of men tabulating the schedules of airplanes falling from the sky; 1920s accounts proving we are on the inside of the earth's crust and the stars we see are peepholes to the outside, deliriums, fevers, phobias, and charts to read the end of the world from certain clues in the Book of Daniel.

"I fear lest someone may expect me to describe exactly what I mean by 'henid,' " Weininger writes. "The wish can come only from a misconception. The very idea of a henid forbids its description; it is merely a something." Further, to sample briefly *Sex and Character*: "The relation between the continuity of memory and the desire for immortality is borne out by the fact that woman is devoid of the desire for immortality. . . . Women are as much afraid of death as are men, but they have not the longing for immortality." And: "We may not give, with certainty, a conclusive answer to the question as to the giftedness of the sexes: there are women with undoubted traits of genius, but there is no female genius, and there never has been one (not even among those masculine women of history which were part) and *there never can be one.*"

He speaks of the "soullessness of women" and "lower-grade consciousness," and in a representative claim he says, "It is only women who demand pity from other people, who weep before them and claim their sympathy." And "The shamelessness and heartlessness of women are shown in the way in which they talk of being loved." He says that women love being mesmerized, with the sly caution that this mustn't be exaggerated.

I can't know how serious Isaac was about the erratic young man who had blazed so brilliantly with one book, attracted crackpots in his time, and vanished except as a curious antifeminist name in a nasty time marching to meet its destiny. I know that when I asked him about it again Isaac *said* he was serious, but I do not think he ever remotely understood Weininger's antisemitism.

There was, as I observed him, an innocuousness to Singer's acceptance of ideas. The turgid inadequacies of his various systems of thought—even, perhaps, a Weininger somewhere in the mix—never really touched what I considered a remarkably delicate balance in him. He was, unless pushed in certain areas, the most inoffensive of men. He made jokes, he struck poses.

He spoke of communism in the 1980s as if college students were currently bedeviled by it. He was, despite his lack of disciplined reading, a truly bookish man, perennially troubled by the world when he looked up from a page of printed matter. Weininger, seemingly an "influence," could be like the hodgepodge of Sherlock Holmes and Jack London and Stanislaw Reymont and his brother, Joshua, who contended for primacy in his mind. He told me—as far as the matter went—that the greatest influence on him, aside from his brother, had been Dostoyevski.

When I asked Singer once about the gruesome effects and subjects in his stories—did they bother him personally with their terror?—he said, laughing, "I'm like the grave digger, it's my business. Why should I be bothered? I write about terrible things. The grave digger makes three dollars a grave, I fill up a few pages."

Listening to his tone, I recognized the prepared answer: it was true as far as it went. But as a person, removing him from the detachment he felt as a writer, I knew him to be bothered—extraordinarily so—by the perverse or grotesque in life. Even superstitious about hearing things discussed.

Talking one day about the rich and poor—a favorite subject of mine that elicited some marvelously queer responses from a writer of such breadth—I said, "So the poor waiter when he doesn't like your tip from another visit to his restaurant, your looks or your manners, or maybe he's black or angry about being poor and you looking like you're rich, he spits in your soup for revenge. Or plain malice."

Aghast, Singer said, "Such a thing could never happen."

"Of course, it could. I've heard people who work in restaurants brag."

"They're criminals." His face was flushed, alternately angry and incredulous—at me, at the waiters.

"What other revenge do they have?" I asked.

He was enraged. "They are worse than murderers," he said, shaking.

"Different values," I said. "They laugh about it among themselves."

"I would give them the electric chair," he said, "you hear, the same as murderers!"

I desisted. We had left the security of print and literature. Life had knocked too loudly at our door. Jupiter's manageable perversities were blessedly far away.

For all of Alma's genteel manner, she could become a tiger in a moment as her mood changed. Threatened, she became imperious. Once, in a booth at Danny's, she persistently adjusted a sweater she carried around her shoulders, rearranging it by throwing it back to achieve a desired effect. Each time she twirled the sweater to get it just right around her shoulders she brushed a woman sitting in the booth behind her. I watched the toss, the woman's head jerk each time she was struck. The woman, a fairly common type in Danny's, not young, had a coiffure that was, I suppose, her main interest in life, and Alma was not so much destroying it as not respecting it.

Finally, I leaned forward and said softly, "Alma, you're hitting that woman with your sweater every time you adjust it."

"What woman?"

Alma turned to glare at the woman in the booth behind her. "Is she complaining?" she asked.

"She's not calling the police," I said.

"Police?" Isaac asked, quickly looking about. "Police? What police? You're saying police?"

"No, it's a joke," I said.

Alma said loudly, "If she doesn't like it she can tell me. She doesn't have to signal you."

"She wasn't signaling me."

Over her shoulder, Alma glared at the woman again. The woman stared back. Alma removed her sweater and passed it across the table to me. "You see this," she said. "The sweater is cashmere. Feel."

"You said police," Isaac said. "What police?"

"A cashmere sweater never hurt anybody," Alma said. "If she's looking for trouble she'll find it."

"She's not looking for trouble," I said.

"She doesn't have to be so delicate," Alma said, swiveling to measure the woman with one last glance.

Another time, again sitting in Danny's with both Alma and Isaac—he tried to avoid this trio, for obvious reasons—I remarked that I had been late for breakfast because it was raining.

"Why should that make you late?" Alma asked.

"The highway's wet," I said. "It took me forty-five minutes to get here."

"Lester, you're not sitting out in the rain on the highway," she said, laughing at me. "Why should a wet highway make you late? There's a roof on your car."

"People drive slower when it's wet," I said. "They're afraid of skidding."

"Skidding?" she asked, laughing again. "A car has rubber tires. People wear rubber soles when they don't want to skid. What are you talking about?"

"It's not me," I said. "I'm not afraid of skidding. I'm not afraid of anything at all. I drive sixty miles an hour in the rain. Other drivers are afraid; they drive slow because they're afraid of skidding. They made me late."

"I never heard of such a thing," she said.

"It's a well-known fact," I said. "People drive slower in the rain."

Isaac clutched his head, quite seriously, in turmoil. "You two will drive me crazy," he said. "I'm going to run from this place."

"Dooly," she said, "Lester says it rains in his car."

He laughed quickly. "So let it rain in his car. It's dry in here," he said. "Stop arguing, you two."

After a few minutes, Alma asked, "Does it rain in your car?"

"It does not," I said. "It rains on my car and on the highway."

She shook her head, sorry for me. "Look out the window," she said. "Those people are running in the rain. Rain makes people hurry. How can you be late because it's raining? I never heard such a thing."

"You're right," I said.

"See, Isaac," she said, "I was right."

The pressures on Alma to retain a sense of her own social elevation, often grand, sweeping, and ultimately ludicrous, against the counterweight of Isaac's gestures toward gratuitous anarchy eventually exhausted her. Maintaining him, with his drive to find and render the paradoxical in even the smallest situation or verbal exchange, was simply impossible. He would seize bread crumbs from a dirty table where all three of us sat; eat half-gnawed rolls left by a former tenant of a booth; drop his arm obliviously into spilled water; and without glancing once at the contents of a cup swallow almost any liquid he found on a table. He would retreat into a corner of a couch when an evening went on too long for him, not unpleasant in his manner, often opening a book to read; and then when Alma left the room he would spring to life as if it had been she who bored him. He seemed to enjoy his role as someone off reading in a corner and listening to others talk; he often looked up to add comments. On the whole, it was always an exasperated Alma who reminded him of the hour, gave him small packages to carry, which he seldom lost but then searched for all through his days in frantic apprehension.

She told me she had tried to take him to an opera once but he had sat for a few minutes listening and then bolted to the rear of the theater, where he paced until she came to retrieve him. He was the active, imaginative child who was dangerous because he would not heed traffic, a burden because he'd lose himself without resources in a crowd and knew no street addresses, phone numbers, or names of cities.

Walking with him to class or back at the university—where lurching from my side he ran into empty classrooms, offices, men's or women's toilets—I asked him, calmly, "Why don't you just walk with me? I'm going the same place you are."

"I think I recognize the room where we're going and I go there," he said.

Eventually, I stood guard outside men's rooms where he went, knowing he would dash from the room out into a corridor, swinging first to the left, then the right, and flying madly in haste in a random direction crying plaintively, "Dr. Goran! Dr. Goran!"

One or two of my colleagues, fair mimics, came to greet me after a time in ill-considered jocularity with his doleful, "Dr. Goran! Dr. Goran!" It was the same lament he uttered in class when he found me gone and stopped everything until I could be located, interrupting and quizzing students about me as they read their short stories, unsatisfied and running out into the corridor calling my name and generous title. The doctorate was a gift from him alone. When I explained I had no such degree, he smiled and said, "So I'll make you a doctor." He never dropped it; I was never sure he understood.

Alma found one day a misspelling in a story I had copyedited. Isaac was devouring the story at the table as if it were someone else's Danish, and, smiling, pleased, he said to me, within her hearing, "She has the eyes of an eagle." Under his breath, he murmured to me, "And she has the brain of an eagle."

Ultimately, I became the referee between them as she hurriedly whispered to me that she could not live another day with him, that he had gone mad. He, in turn, told me weekly he would commit suicide if she persisted in her trials to his rationality. He was willful and vagrant. She was steadfast.

In an American context, battling Alma for the proprieties in Surfside, Singer was a singular figure, but I suspect I would have found him unique if I had been working as a pale, forelocked boy in a kosher butcher shop on Krochmalna Street in Singer's Warsaw and he had been a customer.

The food at Singer's condominium one night when Deedee and I were invited for dinner was fine. The brisket was tender and the bread was fresh and plentiful. But the cork stuck in the wine bottle and none of us could remove it. Isaac watched as everyone in turn tried to extract the broken cork. I knew him well enough to know that his sad smile as he watched me meant Jews had no business bothering with alcohol or that Americans in general wasted their time on wine—for, since Alma wanted desperately for the night to be a success, everything would, in the mystical order of things, fail.

The cork is perhaps still lodged in the bottle.

Walking to the kitchen from the table, with its white tablecloths, napkins, good silverware, and goblets, Alma stopped each time to take from a bowl on a small table a piece of pastry with her as she left the room. The pastries were ruggulach and tiny Danish with almonds. She did not offer anyone else the pastry. She ate the cookies in the kitchen and came back empty-handed.

I watched her make several trips and said, as the evening closed, "Is that pastry for everyone?"

She looked at me directly. I was there as a witness to Alma's ability to hostess a fine evening.

The evening had been put together not for me but for Deedee. Alma sent her cards and stamps from Switzerland, a clear, heart-shaped candle holder, and she brought her small costume jewelry from her European visits. She called my wife fairly frequently for lunch. A cynic might think she wanted transportation from my wife on her errands, but I think she genuinely liked her.

"Why do you want pastry with meat?" Alma asked me.

"Maybe later," I said.

We were not offered pastry later. We also were not offered any of the miniature chocolate bars Alma, in passing, scooped that night from another adjoining bowl on her route to the kitchen.

I have thought about Alma as a guest in our classes, a hostess in her condominium, an imperious diner in seedy restaurants, and a fallen daughter of a silk merchant in Weimar Germany. Thought of her in those moments when she was most herself. And I have come to the conclusion that she had come to think she was invisible, or at best an amorphous shadow diffused through contradictory lights.

A Bach, she told me, her family was well known and wealthy in Germany, renowned clothing manufacturers. She spoke of opera, art galleries, nobility, the easy passage of a youthful heiress to a stable fortune, the road to Surfside from a Bavarian girlhood by green mountainsides and snow-capped peaks. But the links had been cruelly broken by, to use a comprehensible shorthand, the Twentieth Century. She, like Isaac, was—with millions—its victim. She was an ambiguous afterthought to Isaac, to add to her woes.

In a story in the *Miami Herald*, about the time of the dinner where she moved like a wraith among private pastries and miniature chocolates as her guests watched with first amusement, then empty awareness, she was quoted: "I've purposely stayed away from this [writing or keeping a journal] because it's not good to be a shadow, to be rated far below Isaac, and naturally it would have to be that. When you are faced with a situation like mine you make the best of it. Sometimes you feel left out of things—but what can you do? It's just so . . ."

Holding on desperately to continuities with his own past, Singer was capable of trampling the contemporary people and places around him with a disdain as acute as if all that was not prewar Poland was poison ivy. He could settle and lay to rest any number of demons in his fiction with his biting wit and leave the reader charmed; but in the current air he breathed was a suspicion of contagion, and he ran from it, ignored it when he could not fly, and roiled. Alma and her children were among his main targets, omnipresent menaces who with nameless others would eradicate his hard-won literary reputation.

Alma and Isaac Singer at their dining-room table in their condominium in Surfside (1984). Courtesy of the *Miami Herald*.

When we departed that night, we were sad because Alma had tried so hard. We shook hands formally at the door. Each to each.

Isaac was particularly withdrawn. He liked us, my wife and me, generally. He wanted Alma to be happy. It should have been a good night. He did not know what to do emotionally with an experience that did not allow his consuming despair to search out paradoxes for exercises of the reposte, the rejoinder, the quip, and the aphoristic witticism. He had tried; it was leaden. It sounded rehearsed. He sat like a child, solitary, munching a forbidden spiritual cookie with a sense about him that no one loved him. "I think I'll leap in moments from the balcony" was in his dourful manner as he stood to bid us a formal goodbye.

Wasn't this all—the world, universes—going to end soon enough?

A shattered kidney, another Hitler, a disease not in medical books, and, finally, fog—all to be dissipated only by the recitation of another right and honest story by Isaac Bashevis Singer.

All the while the worst demon of all, old age, showed its bared teeth, and Isaac and Alma trembled before the coming onslaught. He spoke to me often of old age as the idea he hated more than any other in his life, and Alma tried with hesitation to bring up the subject when she was alone with me but always rejected what I said as being too grim. What had happened to other people could not happen to her—or Isaac. She was of a better class. Alma fought their destiny as it descended on them as if it were one final uncomprehending critic with a mixed review. She pooh-poohed, derided, and finally dismissed the horror altogether.

After losing himself on the campus with an unfamiliar student guide, Singer asked me, gravely, "Where do you go when you disappear?"

Thinking he was being whimsical, I said, "I'm where I'm supposed to be."

"The classroom is moved somewhere," he said. "You all disappeared."

"You just looked in the wrong place."

"No, I was where I should be. I went to the right place. You disappear all the time."

Singer resolved all the confusion about others' conduct by simply believing—finally—they disappeared. Invisibility was a better answer to incomprehensibility than admitting confusion in understanding someone else.

He was frequently confused about why people did what they did. It was not just American customs. Europe bewildered him too. Is it possible to write of a love affair without the author understanding love—even the love between his own characters? Or is love or hate so generic that what one says about people in love is never wrong?

When I asked him where does Herman Broder go when he just seems to vanish at the end of *Enemies,* he did not understand my question.

"Did you mean he dies?" I finally asked. "It's not clear."

"Of course, he dies," Singer said. "Everybody dies."

When Singer made little sense of what was happening around him, he stabbed into the dark: in his conjecture he might strike a truth.

"The blonde woman, she is your lover?" he asked one week, sitting on the stone bench where the limousine driver left him to wait for me (usually five minutes, which he insisted was half an hour). He had been thinking about the subject of the blonde woman all week, or perhaps she had occurred to him with an urgency on the ride from Surfside.

"I have no lovers in our classes," I said. "Isaac, you're impossible."

Walking along a brisk three feet every three minutes, he stopped and turned to me, peering up. "She called you 'darling' last week," he said.

"She despises me," I said. "She loathes me. 'Darling' was a sign of her contempt for me, a word to make fun of me. She teaches courses here and she and I don't agree on her writing. She's not as good as she thinks."

"It slipped out from her," he said, now not moving even the three feet every three minutes. "She called you 'darling.' "

"She hates me," I said. "Calling a teacher 'darling' in class is a sign of disrespect."

He made a reconciliatory sound. "Not such disrespect," he said. "It's not a vulgar word."

"Used like she did it's vulgar."

"You don't like her writing?"

"I like it okay, but I'm not overwhelmed. If I loved it she'd want me to adore it, say prayers to it."

"She's pretty? You think she's pretty?"

"Some days she looks beautiful."

"And you know her well?"

"Not well, only what she tells me. She says wild things about men she's known."

"She lies?"

"I don't know, what do lies matter to a writer?"

"But she calls you 'darling'?" he persisted.

"You heard her."

"She's your lover," he said emphatically. He walked faster, reassured. He had warmed up for the profundities ahead of us in another class of English 560. My jaw hurt from where I forced a smile. My neck ached.

He said no more on the subject that day, content in his judgment. His withdrawal into his own world could be so satisfying and so self-sustaining that often I had to make him aware of huge crevices in his path. He never saw, lost in his certainties, crackling electrical lines that appeared like magic before him.

"There's a young woman in the class," I said to him that semester. "She's disturbed."

"Disturbed? She's going to talk to the President?" The "President" of the university was an omnipotent figure in his imagination, fearsome and messianic.

"No," I said, "mentally disturbed. Not bothered about our teaching."

"*Misugheh?*"

"Yes, crazy."

"A crazy person?"

"Yes, she's in a bad way. I want you to be careful. Be polite if she raises her hand. I'll call on her."

"How do you know this about her?"

"She claps her hands after you talk, and when I start to talk she stands up and walks around the room."

He shrugged his shoulders. "Maybe you shouldn't talk so much."

"She'd do something else."

"Listen, don't talk so much."

"She walks around all period, but mostly she walks around when I talk."

"She walks where?"

"Between the rows, up and down, in between the chairs."

He looked into my face, searching my motives. "Why does she do that?" he asked. "A person walks, they walk somewhere."

"Because she's mentally unbalanced," I said slowly, "she walks nowhere. She stands and she has no expression on her face and she walks aimlessly."

"She walks toward me?"

"No, she walks around aimlessly, she applauds. Once or twice she walked out of the room altogether."

"You know more than I do about these things, my friend," he said. "I don't know which lady it is. I'll be truthful."

Later the student disappeared from class, and then about six months later sent me a sad apologetic letter explaining that she was probably never going to return to Miami. A letter of evasions and euphemisms but the truth of her confinement apparent, I read it to Isaac. He listened and became angry.

"Why did you let her in class?" he asked.

"There's no way I could tell about her condition at the time," I said.

"I think you attract crazy people," he said.

"You told her her story was very good," I said. "Her story made no sense."

"You know," he said, recovering his poise, "sometimes a crazy person can write very well, it's a fact. But, please, Lester, be more careful." His voice fell to a low plea. "I wouldn't know what to do with a crazy person."

"I'll take care of everything," I said.

"I have to trust you. The President knows?"

"You won't be harmed."

"Please," he said. "You know, you are very good with these crazy people. I can't tell one from another."

I never discussed with him the conditions of life as an academic at an American university. He had a peculiar notion of it, garnered from conversations and courses he had "taught" at other schools. (At one, he told me, he was met weekly by a student and led to a cellar.) His appearances on platforms in school auditoriums, his jokes arranged, his ironies laid out according to subject had not prepared him for the students, faculty, and administrators he met in their earthly daily passage at the university where we worked.

In the middle of March 1981, the university held its first Honors Convocation. Singer was to be the speaker, given the first award. While the honors students were assembled, faculty and university dignitaries given seats of prominence, I introduced Singer to Howard Schnellenberger, the football coach, who had brought—in shirts and ties—his splendid football team.

Singer took the stage before almost a thousand people. "I do not have a degree from a university," he said, "so I am not really a college professor. But I have gone to a university and the university is Dr. Lester Goran. Every week I come and I learn. He is a great teacher. Now, he *is* a teacher! He should get this award, not me."

He went on for ten minutes; mercifully, I have forgotten all but the beginning. I stood on a landing with Bill Babula. He doubled over with laughter. Breaking off occasionally, he said, "It's all right, really, it's all right, Les." He could not contain himself.

Singer's public eulogy had all the high seriousness of a failed fraternity prank. I stepped back into a corridor where I was partially hidden to the people who had turned to watch my reaction to my self-seeking.

"It's all right," Bill said. "I don't hate you. Maybe they'll give you a plaque, too."

"At midnight," I said. "In the dark."

The next day I received a rare telephone call from Singer at my office at the university. Admitting I was at school every day, teaching other classes, would have been to acknowledge that my life flourished outside the town limits of his fictions.

Alma was on the phone first, and she said, "Lester? Wait! Isaac wants to talk to you." Sometimes when she called she said, "Lester, it's Alma Singer, wait!"

"Hello, my friend."

"Hello, Isaac."

"I told them yesterday, yes."

"You did," I said, "and I appreciate your kindness. It was very thoughtful of you."

"Well, you are the professor, not me."

"We do well together," I said. My annoyance with him subsided. He insisted after all that he was no teacher; it was only when he was caught weekly in the moment in a classroom that he became gripped by the fancy that he was and betrayed himself.

I dreaded our working Mondays, which routinely destroyed my affection for him. My mother once, sighing, said, "I wish I had a million dollars," and when I asked, "What would you do with it?" she said, "I'd give it to you." I think Singer, too, at that time in our friendship, would have given me imaginary millions and I was still his captive.

"Tell me," he asked on his call to school, after ensuring my future, "you will be a dean now?"

"No," I said, "I'm where I want to be. I'm a full professor. I can't go any higher."

"A dean is not higher?"

"I don't want to be a dean," I said. "It's another kind of job."

"Full professor," he asked, "what is it?"

"Next to God."

"No, really, don't joke."

"It's the highest rank a professor can reach. I've been a full professor for seven years."

"Seven years? You were a professor before I came?"

"Isaac, I was here nineteen years before you came. I've published eight novels since I came to the university."

I deplored my testiness with him. I still aspired to the literary sanctity of the Isaac Bashevis Singer of my idealizations—writing alone and eloquent, truthful, and imaginative in Olympian reserve.

When he did not respond immediately, I said, "I'm sorry, Isaac, it's just that sometimes I feel as though I'm talking to myself when I talk to you about school and my work here."

Singer asked, "Will they give you tenure now?"

"I have tenure, Isaac," I said. "I've had tenure for thirteen years. I told you that."

"You have tenure?"

"Yes, thirteen years."

"Tell me, my friend, will they give me tenure?"

"No, that's not your situation. You're a Distinguished Professor."

"Oh, then they can fire me?"

"Not likely, if you want to stay."

"Does Saul Bellow—where he is—does he have tenure?"

"Chicago," I said. "I don't know whether he has tenure or not."

"They won't fire him," he said before he hung up.

Stiffness, pride, and the promise of his quick wit characterized Isaac Singer when he posed for the camera. He barely glanced at pictures of himself before turning abruptly away at what he saw. Courtesy of M. L. Carlebach.

∼ PART TWO

"Ladies, There Are No Rules"

Chapter Three

MY LIFE AND its shadings, familiar enough to sociologists and novelists of the cityscapes of the thirties, forties, and fifties, remained an enigma to Singer. Usually a very polite man, he could elaborately and theatrically demonstrate indifference by sinking his chin into his neck or making a sound near disgust and waving away something one said as trite or obvious. For Isaac the mystery in me was in the daily life and sensibility I employed in my mundane affairs: he claimed he had read several of my works and had nothing, nothing at all, to say about them. I doubt he read anything of mine except a review of him. He had never read Twain, Hawthorne, Melville, Faulkner, Bellow, James, Fitzgerald, John Cheever, or Flannery O'Connor either. Reading other peoples' fiction was not where his strength lay. His enormous resources for sympathetic rendering into fiction such varieties of human experience came from his early reading and observations from life. He confirmed from nature what he had apparently believed from childhood and dismissed it when it went against the grain of his understanding of things.

I asked him once, "Would you be able to work with me if I were a famous writer?"

He said, "You are the first real writer I've worked with."

"I mean famous," I said, "well known."

He simply said, "No," embarrassed, I think.

He valued me not as a fellow writer but as a curiosity of how the writer of marginal acclaim gets through life without prizes of adulation or money, with merely the sense of his connection to things based on writing about them. He constantly reassured me—I didn't need these endorsements either—that he had been as unknown once as I and that I would one day come to fame. I do believe before we were through with each other he came to recognize that there are degrees and sides to fame and even comparative comfort with oneself not predicated by being defined by other people. He was, for all his insight, trapped in the European groove of respect for titles: "Professor," "Dean," "President," "little seamstress," "beggar," "baker," "squire." So precarious was Singer's hold on what he saw as his own rank that when he saw me with a black-jacketed copy of Alfred Kazin's *New York Jew* he asked angrily, "Why do you carry around a book like that? Do you know what people think when they see a title like that on a book?"

I know that in certain moods Singer observed everything, and I wasn't surprised to look up often in a crowded room and find his eyes in narrow slits watching me. Once, after one of these under-the-microscope sessions, he said to me after class at the door of his waiting car, "You are very good with women."

Thinking it nonsense, I asked, "To what do you attribute my charm?"

He shook it off, annoyed at the question. "You are tall and clever," he said, liking his judgment well enough that he repeated it in a friendly tone.

Another time, sitting in Danny's Restaurant, I teasingly untied the bow in the back of the apron of a waitress we saw weekly. She laughed and patted me on the cheek and said, "Be careful of what you'll find there." She was perhaps in her middle sixties, thin, her face lined with fatigue but always friendly.

When she left, Singer exploded. "That woman!" he said, marveling. "She would have slapped me in the face and I would have felt it a year later."

"I'm sorry I did that. I should have been punched. It was a stupid thing to do."

"But she patted your face and laughed. She would have hit me."

"I assure you I never did anything like it before and I won't do it again."

He sat back. "Women always talk to you."

"If you mean students," I said, "sometimes they think it won't hurt their grades."

He could never understand that what he thought of as our mystical popularity in class might be from other sources than our galvanizing academic abilities.

"No," he said, "I see the way they talk to you. Everybody talks to you."

He meant, I think, "and you're nobody famous."

"I guess you're right," I said, "but I talk to everybody too. I embarrassed one of my sons one time when he and I took a bus trip. It was night and the bus was almost empty. Bobby was dozing so I fell into a conversation with a black man sitting in the back of the bus, and he had a bottle in a brown paper bag so we had a few drinks. It was a bus to Pittsburgh, and it turned out I'd gone to high school with his brother."

Singer sat back with eyes once more half closed. "I couldn't do that," he said. "I'm too shy."

"It's not a habit," I said.

Singer made a sound in his throat, light pitched, almost keening. He rocked slightly. "I'm so alone," he said. "I'm alone, I'm alone."

"Isaac, that's foolishness."

"Come, we'll walk," he said. He recovered quickly. "I'll tell you about the Warsaw Writer's Club."

While I was still moved by Singer's writing, I could not sustain my enthusiasm for fiction confined, compressed, locked away, and evaded in our classes. I had come to teaching from door-to-door sales in Pittsburgh; being a college professor with him was now a reversion to the scams and deceits I had promised myself I would drop the day my first novel was accepted for publication. The Academy had been for me a retreat from double-dealing and side-of-the-mouth gymnastics. But my years of background in the depths left me with no false sense of where I was. Universities have their fair share of snake-oil hucksters in all ranks, and creative writing is a fragile camel, indeed, by which to send academic or artistic expectations across the desert.

Add to the sly open-sesame of someone purporting to make writers of fiction as effectively as other teachers might turn out accountants and dentists down the hall the weight of Isaac Singer maintaining a classroom confidence game within the broader game itself (to say nothing of "higher education" altogether), and I faltered under the burden.

"Bill," I said to my chairman in February 1981, "I want out of this with Singer." Bill Babula was shopping about for a new job, soon to leave for a position as dean of arts and humanities at Sonoma State in Santa Rosa, California.

"I know," Bill said, unhappy for me. "But I don't know what to do. What about you supervising a grad student to work with him?"

"That'll give me two jobs instead of one with him."

"He won't go for a woman to work with him?"

"He'd feel degraded at the suggestion."

"Les, it's a problem. We can't lose him. Do you want to go down in history as the guy who lost Isaac Singer?"

"Not if I can shift the loss to you, Bill."

"I'll think of something," he said, but he didn't as the days passed in the spring of 1981.

The chairman, for all his concern, could do nothing for me. Built into the system was the belief that a man with Isaac Singer's manifold credentials in creating novels, short stories, and essays could talk nonsense or wisdom, reveal secrets of what lay at the core of his genius or choose to hold back the merest hint of who he really was, and no one would dream of holding him accountable. His was the only picture of a Miami faculty member to run on television during a famous postseason football game (a fact I was reminded of the day after by other faculty members). His photo was on the cover of fund-raising pamphlets. One hundred twenty-five scholarships for honors students were awarded annually in his name.

Yet all the while he announced periodically to our coeducational classes, ignoring the young men, "Ladies, there are no rules. This is the only true rule about writing."

To counter his sense of there being only women in our classes, I moved our class from a small conference room to a regular classroom, where he could be seated somewhat back from the awareness of pressing femininity around our long table that disturbed and provoked him. It was no good. Here he couldn't hear the questions or really see anyone beyond the front row. We went back to the conference room the next semester.

It's true that Singer made an occasional attempt to cite a contemporary name brand, the qualities of an American politician, or express some arcane information about the present, but mostly he dwelled with his memories.

He told a student to call the vehicle in his story an automobile, not a Mercedes. "In five hundred years no one will know what a Mercedes is," he said. "How many people today ever heard of such a car?"

My face contained multitudes of no meaning as the student stared at me.

For months Singer had been talking to me in 1981—I thought in general terms—of a certain lawyer, whose name I never asked, who was going to ruin him. He complained that his publishers pushed other writers instead of him. Leaving no one out of the conspiracies against him, he said *The New Yorker* was communistic. He insisted that this demonic lawyer was going to shame his long literary career. We talked often about the large body of work he had serialized in the *Forward* that had never been translated from Yiddish. He said there was a long novel, *Shadows on the Hudson*, in Yiddish and a book about two gangsters still untranslated. These works did not bother him. He was concerned about works he considered trashy, things written under the names Isaac Warshovsky and Isaac Bashevis decades ago. He finally asked me if I would make sure that these things never saw the light of day in English or any other language.

"How bad can they be?" I asked.

"Trash," he said, "garbage like you've never seen."

"Isaac, you're exaggerating."

"No, sentimental, foolish. It would hurt me if these things were published after I die."

"What do you want me to do?"

"It must be fast," he said. "It must be this week." He wanted me to call an attorney of my own choosing in Miami and have myself named his literary executor. Isaac's panic was inescapable. I felt something imminent.

I called the attorney most people in Miami at that time would summon, Dick Gerstein. Known for reliability, probity, and imagination, Gerstein had been state attorney for twenty years in Dade County, winning elections in easy walks, and was now in private life. An old friend, I admired him professionally and personally.

Looking into it, Gerstein said there was no provision in the law that someone could be simply named a "literary executor." It was executor of his will and estate, nothing less. The prospect was not appealing. Singer kept sums of money in numerous banks, mysterious and vague, and traveled to Switzerland annually, occasionally Brazil or Argentina, and had no investments, he told me, except passbooks. I had no idea of what was expected of an executor, but I agreed to take on the role of literary executor. He insisted I become executor of his estate upon his death. "Listen, you are my one friend," he said. "You must do this for me. I have reasons."

"Am I ever going to hear these reasons?" I asked. "Will you tell me what you want done? What's the purpose of this will anyhow? What's bothering you?"

"You'll read the will, you'll read the will when I die."*

I agreed to undertake being executor if he'd agree that Dick Gerstein be the coexecutor. Gerstein, who had been shot down over Germany on his twenty-first birthday, was the most resourceful man I knew; it would take a Gerstein to unravel the devious

---

* I heard nothing further about this will or its contents. Apparently, according to a later will Singer drew up in 1984, I was not a "literary executor." But by the time I heard, it was 1991 and he had died and the alarms and dilemmas of 1982 had long been replaced for Singer with other dramas.

financial labyrinths Isaac had burrowed in his innocence and cunning.

We went to the offices of Harold Kassewitz, another Miami synonym for evenhandedness and honorable practice. On the elevator up to Kassewitz's office, Singer said, "I don't want Alma's children to receive a penny of the money. Not a penny!"

"Won't Alma give it to them?" I asked. "Or don't you intend to leave her anything?" When he became drawn into himself, I stopped him by taking his arm. "Isaac, are you going to leave Alma out of your will?"

"I'll give her one third," he said. "Not a penny to her children."

He was silent, and we walked down to the attorney's office.

Singer ignored Gerstein. Gerstein was a very tall, formidable figure, somber in appearance but actually boyish in his enthusiasm and humor. Singer practically refused to shake hands with him, a response I think he followed in his caricaturist's mind of reacting to other people's physicality, as if those were clues to their spiritual natures.

After introductions, I sat in Kassewitz's office with Singer. Kassewitz was himself about Isaac's age. Kassewitz asked, "How large is the estate?" and Isaac answered and I quickly stood. This was none of my affair.

Singer motioned me to sit back down, and I said, "No, I'll wait outside." The sum was three times larger than I had casually estimated; I felt that hearing details, some of which were to be awful, if I knew the mind of my friend, would not be spiritually or physically healthy for me.

I had spent the spring vacation at home with my arm in a sling with an undiagnosable pain in my right shoulder and upper pectoral. My arm still ached.

Singer sat quietly in the car on the trip back to his condominium. He was at peace. "I left my son a third too," he said.

We rode silently, once more trapped in a web of denunciations and ancestral Polish-Jewish enmities from the Yiddish typewriter of a great writer.

He called me at home that night, April 7.

"Well, it's done, my friend."

"I hope you feel better."

"You will be left a nice sum."

"Isaac, you didn't have to do anything like that."

"Twenty thousand dollars!" He is pleased, his voice is exuberant. "Twenty thousand is good, yes?"

"Princely."

"Goodbye, my friend. We will work together."

I knew enough never to bring the subject up again.* To talk of it with my family is to awaken the sleeping angels of death hovering around the idea of a will. I am embroiled in a war. The enemy is faceless. And what of the distribution of the money from his estate? The subject of Singer's will and my responsibilities gives me a small ache over my right eye every time I think of it. I see in my future not another semester or two with Isaac Singer: I see court cases and long acrimonious letters to the *New York Review of Books.* I see strangers issuing intemperate remarks directed at my own work and character, and me responding with scathing challenges to anyone who would defile Isaac Singer's career or doubt my integrity. It is not work I am cut out for.

I have taken a one-day, good-intentioned, help-your-neighbor bus ride into unfamiliar territory; now I want to get back on the bus. The hermetically sealed world of Isaac Singer—complete and airless, no art or architecture in it, no room in it for anyone else's fiction or music or film—bores and frightens me in its emptiness. His richness of sensitivity is all in his prose fiction. And I am now his defender forever because he loves and trusts me.

I paced around our house for two days, sleepless, and then my wife, whom Singer enjoyed and honored because she was handsome, soft-spoken, and open in her affection for him, said, "Lester, Isaac

---

* Whatever the contents of Singer's most recent will, the twenty-thousand dollars he spoke of remain with my mother's fanciful million. I think of both sums as love offered in a time of good feelings for me.

Singer is going to live a long time. He's Isaac Singer, remember? There are going to be twenty wills after this one and twenty executors." Calmer, I saw things in the larger perspective and almost slept well, except for the pain in my shoulder.

On April 22 with Singer back in New York, I went with Bill Babula for the last time to Nassau in the Bahamas. The university had a joint teaching program with the University of the Bahamas, and Bill and I had been flying over every other Saturday for years during the alternate semesters we taught creative writing. There were usually so many students signing up for the course—fifty-five or so—that the class was split up, Babula taking one section and I another. With regard to the number of aspirants toward literary achievement, David Segal, my late editor at McGraw-Hill, told me a parable about publishing. "Imagine," he said, "a situation where there are millions of herring in the sea and hundreds of fishermen out to catch the herring. Then hundreds of other people are employed on shore to can the herring and others working to design the labels for the cans; and there are thousands of other people working in the supermarkets to stock the shelves with the cans of herring. But *nobody eats herring.* That's the situation with publishing fiction."

Some of the joys of teaching in the Bahamas lay for me in the sweep to the island coast of the sometimes-large L1011 Bill and I rode virtually alone at eight in the morning. Below us, as the airplane came in at eight thousand feet, there lay the blue water, and we could see clearly crabs and fish and coral formations in dizzy patterns. I felt young watching the sun on the water. I luxuriously read all the scores from the day before in the NBA playoff games. I would miss those mornings, and on our last trip before Bill went to California, I looked up from my newspaper to see him observing me. He is fifteen years younger than I. When he read my novel *The Stranger in the Snow*, about the fighting at Anzio during World War II (there was little written on Anzio and the debacle there in 1966, when I published the book), he told me that on the day I described in my novel, before Bill was born, his father had died on the beachhead there.

I said to him on the airplane, guessing at what he was thinking because we seldom discussed the subject now, "Bill, what am I going to do?"

"How many points did Larry Bird have last night?" he asked.

The following Saturday I dreamed of my father calling to me as I was walking down the steps from the third floor in our house in the neighborhood where I was born. "Where are you going?" he asked, and I prepared to say, "Why do you care now? You've never asked before."

I woke suddenly from my argument with my father with a pain in my chest, like a fist pushing up from my abdomen. It settled, hurt more, in my chest and shoulders and neck. I thought, I'm alive; but if I'd died, that recurring dream of walking down those long steps to the streets of my childhood would have been the last thought I had on this earth. My wife drove me to the emergency room of the South Miami Hospital ten minutes away. It was a quarter after four in the morning.

It was not a heart attack but a hiatal hernia on the rampage. The next day, in the course of testing my heart—I stayed in intensive care for eight days—it was discovered that I had two blocked arteries, a situation, as I saw it, as alarming as I chose to make it. But, to add to my problems, I became a walking pharmacy. Whatever the six different varieties of pills and capsules I took through the day did to stabilize my condition, what happened to me consciously was a series of occasional post–intensive care hallucinations that went on for months, even years (alarm clocks singing like voices in Walter Lantz cartoons, Day-Glo numbers over my bedroom door, and a voice here or there reciting James or Browning). The medicine also caused vertigo and tides of desperation fueled by an anti-adrenalin pill. While the pills were forecast for a hundred years into my future, I cut them down, through improving health, to one nonhallucinatory pill a day—not chic and probably ineffective.

I told Isaac about my eight days in intensive care when he came back for his annual fall visit to Surfside in September.

"But you're all right now?" he asked.

"I guess so."

"Good, good, my friend, we'll do much work together," he said.
I had missed our breakfasts and talks. He and his outlandish
passage had become normalcy for me after my brush with eternity—
his familiar face and small, spare body, clean and complete, a mes-
senger from a time when writing fiction was important.

In the hospital and recuperating later, I'd thought a lot about him.
He was a man who wore disorder as familiarly as he did his ancient,
peeling belt. Why condemn him? He was by nature, as he often
confessed, perplexed. He had, I'm sure, no agenda for throwing
situations into disarray. But once the world around him became
confounded with constantly expressed complaints and mystifications,
he thrived. His schemes, I believe, might be logical enough at the
outset; but then the old comforts of bewilderment settled in on him
and he began his cheerful, blundering trip on to the next denoue-
ment. His elfishness allowed him to slip from one misadventure to
the next with little censure from anyone. Although he repeated many
answers to interviews as if he had rehearsed them, I think it was a
thrill to him each time he came up with a sincere spontaneity. He
liked about himself that he did not prepare anything to say: just let it
heroically come. At his best he was like Chesterton or Shaw, turning
the obvious upside down to reveal the paradox in the easily assumed.

Seeing him that fall, I relished the life that flowed from his quick,
impish imagination. At his worst, being with him was an endless skit
with the old vaudeville comics Smith and Dale: thrust, retreat,
parry—insults traded in a gentle, even grudging manner but often
barbed. He made straight men of strangers or "his best friend."

I leaned in close during our reunion in Danny's so as not to miss
a word. Our class was more than three months away; I had before me
a blessed whole semester without him at the university. But I was
fascinated now by the subject we spoke of, the great days in the forties
at the *Forward*. Its rotogravure section floated around our apartment
in my childhood. My mother was their most devoted reader. Isaac

told tales of Abe Cahan, the martinet giant who dominated the Yiddish literary scene for decades and who had written *The Rise of David Levensky*, a well-known book I respected and Isaac hated (as he did anything that touched on his late editor at the *Forward*).

"Cahan used to describe his writers in flattering terms—one was a writer named Botvinick. He called him 'Tolstoy.' Another he said was 'Chekhov.' A third faker he called 'Gogol.' "

"What kind of man was Botvinick?" I asked.

"Botvinick? Botvinick asked me this one time: Who wins a case better, a lawyer who knows the law or one who knows the judge? He meant his relationship with Abe Cahan. If Cahan had told him to tramp on his writing he would have done it. If Cahan gave the word he made changes in his work like a wild man."

"Cahan was strong, wasn't he?" I asked. "Did you make changes at his suggestions?"

"One day, when I was writing *The Family Moskat* I had enough from Cahan," he said, "I told him he should give me a contract or I wouldn't turn in the last four weeks. Cahan said to me: 'There are no contracts for writers in Yiddish.' Well, he gave me a contract and a few weeks later he had a 'seizure.' He never got a chance to attack me or my book in the *Forward*."

Singer was smiling broadly now. He was poised happily for my next question.

"And Botvinick?" I asked.

"Ah, Botvinick," he said, laughing. "He wrote an anecdote for the *Forward* about a truck carrying chickens that was wrecked, and the chickens scattered from the truck in an accident. Botvinick did not say to his readers that the chickens were like the Jews running away from the Nazis. It was an obvious thing. Instead he wrote that the chickens reminded him of the Nazis. The Nazis or the chickens in their scattering from the truck somehow represented food or a product being taken away from the poor in their rush and a loss to the farmer. I don't know what he was talking about. Neither did anyone else."

"What happened to Botvinick?"

"What happens to all of us? He died."

"He didn't write another *War and Peace*."

"He would have called it *Peace and Plenty*."

"Cahan gave you trouble, particularly?" I asked.

"No, he gave everyone except maybe a favorite trouble," Singer said. "He demanded every day of the week changes from me. There's a section in *The Family Moskat* that I wrote in an hour—six pages—to meet a deadline. Every time I look into the book I recognize it."

"Was Botvinick a sort of average writer on the newspaper? I mean, compared to others."

"They were worse. He was like Homer to the rest of them. These writers were not just bad writers. They were primitives. It was like going to Africa and discovering someone there in the wilderness and bringing him to a newspaper and having him write."

"*The Family Moskat* is a wonderful book. How did you survive in such company?"

"My friend, I wrote things sometimes as bad as Cahan's Chekhovs. I wrote terrible things under other names than my own," he said, and I said, "Surely not."

"Ah, foolish coincidences, sentimental lies, characters there never were on heaven or earth. You have to understand the readers didn't want much more from us."

"But my mother always spoke of you. I don't remember hearing much of anyone else."

"Your mother was a sophisticated reader. A reader doesn't have to go to college, you know, to read a book. Your mother had a certain life and it taught her many things and when she read a book she could see things from her life in it."

∽ Chapter Four

IN OCTOBER THAT year Alma called me from her hospital room and asked me if I'd bring Isaac to see her at Mt. Sinai Hospital on Miami Beach. She said she had been stricken by an attack of phlebitis and she wanted to see me and Deedee and did not want Isaac to come alone in a taxicab. After our regular breakfast morning in Surfside on the tenth, Isaac and I drove down to Collins Avenue to visit Alma.

We couldn't find a parking place in the visitor's lot at Mt. Sinai, so I parked in a physician's reserved space. I wrote on a slip of paper "Emergency Visit" and put it under my windshield wiper.

"What did you write?" Singer asked.

"I told them I was a friend of yours."

He laughed. But he was tense. Neither of us liked hospitals. Having spent eight days in late April listening to my heart beat in electronic notes, I hoped to be a while away from the place. Alma was in room 898, bad news from my point of view—an eight-floor elevator ride with Singer, who did not like elevators. As luck would have it, we could not find where the elevators were. We had circled the parking lot until I thought Isaac was going to jump out of the car; and now we walked down one corridor, then another, searching for elevators.

Singer whimsically said over the years that demons unzipped his fly, stole mail (particularly checks), and caused his television to revolve and spin. There was a novel at least the length of *Billy Budd* in Isaac Singer's adventures with the coaxial cable.

His set made unnatural noises, growled, and only with effort (here serious) by Alma or Isaac, who snatched at great peril the cord from the outlet, failed to cause their deaths by electrocution.

"Demons," he said in Yiddish as we walked the corridors. "Ask, please ask someone."

"Isaac, when I see someone I'll ask."

He stopped a black man at a candy machine and in a voice heavy with supplication pleaded, "Where are the elevators?"

The man stopped at the question, considered it, and said in a heavy French accent, "I don't know, but I'll look with you."

Isaac addressed all of his remarks now to the reliable and helpful man, until after a few minutes the two of us finally stumbled onto an elevator. Isaac thanked the man profusely and said to me, "See, you have to ask when you don't know."

We ascended in silence to the eighth floor, where Alma was pleased to see Isaac, less so me. She looked over my shoulder for Deedee.

"She had something to do," I said.

"What do you mean she had something to do? What did she have to do?"

"Bake bread."

"Why is she baking bread?"

"I told her to," I said. "Really, Alma, I don't know what she's doing. She told me to tell you she's sorry, she'll call you."

"Baking bread?" Alma said. "Did you hear, Isaac? Lester said Deedee's baking bread."

When I asked Alma about her phlebitis, she asked, "Who told you I had phlebitis? Who have you been talking to about me?"

"You told me on the phone."

She said, "Well, keep it to yourself. I don't like rumors to start."

After we had been sitting there for a few minutes, Alma, who liked to discuss gossip in the newspapers, asked me what I thought about the story of Governor Hugh Carey's wife, who had apparently been married to two men at the same time. That reminded Isaac of a story.

"In Warsaw," he said, "there was a certain Hasid who married more than one woman, more than two. When the people of the town came to him to complain he told his accusers, 'You are all interested in such things—I am only interested in spiritual things. I don't have time to think of women. I marry them because I'm not concerned with them as much as I am in spiritual matters. My mind doesn't dwell on women: that's why I forget and marry more than one.' "

Jauntily, we left Alma's room, the promise of getting out of the hospital buoying both of us. As we came toward an exit, Isaac dashed into a stairwell on the eighth floor.

I said, "Isaac, there's eight flights of stairs down."

He said, "That's all right, that's all right."

I followed him at his fast rate of descent. He did not trust me to find the elevator down—and who knows, we might not find another Haitian to guide us.

Exhilarated by our quick descent, once outdoors we walked quickly across the parking lot. If I'd been towed, I would call a cab for Singer, though I dreaded the thought of explaining why my car had vanished. But it was there, without a ticket. We drove around the lot for a long time until we found our way back to Collins. Isaac hadn't noticed my peculiar route: with him and his aura of confusion, I had been lost once more in the parking lot of Mt. Sinai.

He was filled with goodwill. It had been a fine visit to a hospital. And it was over. As we drove toward Surfside, he said, "I think I see an organization in the universe. I think the older I get the more I see the order."

"What part does the assassination of Sadat play in the order?" I asked, the premier of Egypt having been killed that week.

"I'll tell you," he said. "A butcher shop is organized, but not for the animals in it. Yet there's an organization to the place. The universe is organized too, but not for mankind." He was silent.

"Does your metaphor about a butcher shop have any further meaning? Do you think the universe is a butcher shop?" I asked.

"Yes."

He was quiet, and then he said, "I'll tell you a story about a man who went to a bank, it was a man like you or me and he asked that he be allowed to deposit his hundred dollars with the president of the bank. He felt that the president could give him more than the 5 percent being given to everyone else. It was explained to him that it was 5 percent for everyone, for him as well as a washerwoman, that a person did not get more by dealing directly with the president. That's the way of the universe. Everyone gets the same, man and animals, no greater rewards for mankind because they communicated with the Almighty, or felt organization around them. It's like knowing that Dostoyevski wrote his books. We can talk about it, but what good does it do us with Dostoyevski? We still don't understand him. That's religion too, talk about what we don't know anything about. Say this, say that. We can say what we want, the books are the books and the universe is itself. What we do is talk about it and what it does is what it wants to do."

"You know, Isaac," I said, "this Almighty of yours doesn't seem to be One a person could love, or even should love."

"That's right," he said. "He does not give mercy. He gives justice."

"Well, I'm a narrow person and I think I want very little—I don't even know what to want—but I think I have something, what little I wanted, maybe exactly all I could want. I call that mercy."

Singer said, "The mercy was that you didn't want much. That's what you got, nothing else. Justice from the Almighty."

We walked for a while in the late, sunny October afternoon and I asked him if he'd like to come home with me for dinner.

"No," he said. "I'm happier here."

"You'll be here without Alma though."

"I have things to do," he said.

I didn't know whether in their unusual marriage he meant that he didn't miss her or that her presence would be with him in their condominium even with her physical absence. It was not a relationship easily understood.

It was a marriage between two independent people often perversely, single-mindedly in pursuit of individual goals. Isaac's demons of record would require elucidation by the very Dr. Freud he so often mocked or by the incomprehensible Dostoyevski; and Alma's direction was Isaac's well-being.

He could reduce her to tears by telling her, "You don't take care of me." And she was not a woman susceptible to weeping. She was, in fact, something of a hard character in Surfside, respected as Isaac's wife but known as picky about seats in restaurants, high-handed in demanding pastries and vegetables in stores, brusque, and peculiar. She had a quick, limping walk—a tall stately woman, nevertheless, making her way on the hour daily to her stockbroker on Harding Avenue and in communication with a variety of accountants. For his part, Isaac spoke of an accountant but vaguely assured me his money was all in savings accounts.

He told me on several occasions he was going to simply run away from her, and sometimes weakly she caught my sleeve and whispered to me that he would soon drive her as mad as he was. But between them there was a touching connection, sympathetic and understanding, secretive, a fortress against the world.

Many years before I met them they bought and collected antique silver candlesticks, trays, artifacts of good design and material. They hid the treasures in their apartment in New York and checked daily to see that they were not disturbed.

The idea of their silver would occur to them while they were out for an evening, and they would break off whatever they were doing and rush home to check their store, always reassured, always together in their clandestine fortune and its protection, united in panic.

I don't know how valuable the silver was; but I know the communion they felt in safeguarding the silver was as precious as a mountain of gold to them. Its secret contentment, its valuable presence, was a balm to both their spirits. Isaac had done well, become world famous, was loved everywhere, but well-being, even before international acclaim, was not unknown to them. They had stocks and passbooks and silver. They would never fall to poverty. They had the silver, like a child, between them and each other to share the treasure. It was there to be remembered, checked and rechecked, a quiet flutter of nightly goodness before they slept.

Though having each other to quarrel with and then side with against real and imagined enemies, each could still be consumed by loneliness. Alma denied it, and Isaac swam as best he could with the terror. "If I could not write," he told me more than once, "I'd kill myself."

At a gathering at the Faculty Club at the university, what had been the usual lighthearted banter by Singer was interrupted when a man in the audience asked, "How does it feel to be seventy-seven years young?"

Singer was in a quick rage. "Don't ask such questions! No one is years young. A man is years old. And it is not a joke. It is nothing to joke about. It is a terrible thing to be old, not a joke." He stood alone in a room of perhaps two hundred people, immersed in the desolation that came from feeling perennially misunderstood. For all the millions of words he had written, he had not communicated his isolation.

Occasionally, people in class took pictures of him. A young man in class with some skills took, from my point of view, several touching portraits and worked at processing them—fine paper, depths and shadows—a tribute to his affection for Singer. The student waited with his proud package to speak to Singer after class and handed Isaac two of his mounted portraits. Singer glanced at them and in an abrupt, almost angry, gesture flung them back across the desk at the student.

"They're for you, Mr. Singer," the student said. "You can keep them."

"I have plenty of pictures," Singer said.

The old man in the picture haunted Isaac Singer and needed no graphic reminders of decrepitude to make itself further known to him.

In 1982 and 1983 a generous but thoughtless gesture of enthusiasm in Singer took on unimagined proportions in our classes. Each year he said, with a light touch, of some story, "If I had a magazine I'd publish this story!" He seldom said it twice in a semester, his memory exquisite over lines that he'd used in class—except at the end—and he'd turn to me in class for my reaction. I'd say, "Not in my magazine, Professor," if the story was desperately bad, or sometimes I'd say, "I'd buy a magazine to publish this story."

Mostly, such fervor for student work on Isaac's part came from his sense of catch-up. If he'd been what he considered too harsh on one story that week or the week before, he'd laud something inane or inept to win back the class he thought he'd lost. His interest was largely in striking a balance that would leave the class liking him. There was sometimes fury in the ranks, or merely confusion, that I'd have to deal with all week long, over why he praised so extravagantly a certain hapless performance. Other words of Singer's appreciation were "This is a unique story from a real writer" and "You will be a writer. I was not such a writer at your age."

Turning to a young man who had lapsed, in my emphatically stated opinion, into incoherence, Singer attempted to comfort him. "How old are you, my friend?" preparing the well-known, "When I was your age . . . "

The young man said, "Thirty-one."

Singer gulped, caught himself, and rocked for a moment. "Well, there's still plenty of time for you to learn how to write," he said.

Out of his undeniable kindness—or perhaps insensitivity to where he was—there grew a strange, unhappy transaction between Isaac and certain students. Quite simply, he promised students, with no consideration of their vaulting ambitions, that he would get them published. This was usually accomplished in the final moments after class when each of us would separately answer questions from students or visitors to the session. He said to various students, "Please give me your manuscript and I will take it to my publisher." I heard him say it easily and thought, "What the hell, it's a crazy thing to do. But the explanations for what happened on the student's march to the Nobel Prize will be up to Isaac Singer." There was always the chance, too, that something good, like a professional reading, might occur, and the student would be that much further ahead. However, the manuscripts vanished the minute Isaac took them from a student. Walking to the car he'd tap himself and ask me, "What did I do with that manuscript?"

Since the exchange was often done in hurried, stolen moments outside of my hearing, I said, "I don't know."

The student, of course, knowing I hadn't been nearly as enthusi-
astic as Isaac Singer about his or her story decided I had done
something to sabotage a career about to take off like a rocket. When
they'd call or visit me after weeks, I'd say, "I don't know about your
story—what does he say?"

"He says you know."

"I don't."

When I confronted him, Singer said, "Please, when I'm gone from
Miami tell them the publisher is holding the manuscript and I can't
get it back. Tell them it takes a long time for a publisher to read a
story."

"Isaac, this is bad business. I don't care about what people think
of our class, but you're hurting these students. They have their hopes
built up. They're going to be disappointed. It's cruel."

"Please, I thought I would show it to my publisher. Listen, Lester,
I lost the story."

"What do you want me to do?"

"Write them a little note and sign it. Say what you want, please."

I wrote little notes. I signed his initials—a practice he never
followed—to render the signature above it only as a device of our
chicanery.

As people thrust manuscripts at him he nodded and accepted them
and I received calls from strangers asking his New York number.
When I could, I collected these stories as soon as they were handed
to him, otherwise—demons! His bland good humor, his wish, I'm
sure, to set these people off on publishing careers was balanced in my
mind with the outraged, teary faces of students condemning me.

A typical note I wrote to one woman who had struck new depths
of inconsequence in class and probably in the clandestine story she
slipped to Singer read:

> Dear Ms. Brown (not her name):
> Your story has much to recommend it, but it just has many things
> missing and they are the things that make a story great. Trust your
> teacher, Mr. Lester Goran, he is a thoughtful man and will not deceive

you. He has nothing to gain by telling you a bad story is good or a good story is bad.

I.B.S.

Singer liked to say to me that he was the good uncle in class and I was the bad uncle, repeating it once or twice to the students themselves. But when I explained to him that what he thought of as "bad" was what the students were paying for, he nodded, let-him-talk.

In our classroom world of us and students, Isaac Singer often did not want to help what he saw as competitors—so intensely was he embroiled in the causes he thought he represented. He withheld his best from our classes and hid and stayed confounded himself, happily or miserably as the occasion fell on him. He dealt with enemy writers out there: poor, ungrammatical, disorderly syntaxed, and faceless and boneless wonders in our classes—or, quite simply, gullible peasants whom one could tell anything with impunity. In this sybaritic and ignorant world of spoiled professors and teachers, he and I had only to be sure no one checked our hours and to have given suitably inflated grades to quiet any complaints.

"Give them all—what is it? As? Give them As, please, my friend."

The sexual content of our female students' stories sometimes escaped him altogether. Of a student story where two obvious lesbians took a bath together, he asked me, "Is she a lesbian, the woman writer?"

I said, "It's what she's interested in writing about."

"She's a lesbian, yes?"

"I don't know, I wasn't in the bathtub."

"You know her?"

"Yes."

"She's a lesbian?"

"I guess so."

"A lesbian. And she's not afraid to write about it?"

"Isaac, there's plenty of books written by lesbians. You know that."

"But to write about it in a class?"

"You mean people will look at her?"

"Yes, people will look at her."

"I didn't see anyone looking at her."

"To tell you the truth, I didn't understand the story either when she read it," he said.

"But now you'll look at her."

"Yes, you'll tell me which one she is—I can't tell one from another. She likes men too, you think? Sometimes a man can change them around."

He took the sexual voices of our women students, outside or in their stories, personally. Very early there was a story from Bess about a defeated young woman who slept around and was, in the old-fashioned term, "taken advantage of." She had a friend named Tom, an old man with whom she drank beer and felt comfortable. He was one of the few people in her world with whom she could laugh easily or talk. At the end of the story, after sex with one of her alley-cat lovers, she lies in bed and cries and wishes she could talk to Tom about her unhappiness.

Singer said he thought the young woman in the story was unbalanced, and I said—this was a high moment in American pedagogy—that I thought the woman was simply numb. Singer then insisted on nymphomania as an explanation.

The student writer said the young woman was nothing of the sort. One woman, then another, said Goran liked the story because the young woman in the story was unhappy in sex and I like unhappy endings for women who have sex. (The first woman called me later and said that she'd had a bad day and her remark had been "off the wall"; I don't think the second woman thought about it much after class, since classes are often unreal and sort of never-happened to some students.)

Singer said, to everyone's embarrassed silence, "You know, young woman, you make fun of the old man in the story . . . "

"She wasn't making fun of the old man," I interrupted.

" . . . and old men are often more robust lovers than young men," Singer said.

Quieted, I said, "I see. Does anyone want to say anything else?"

"It is a fact," Singer said. "It is well known: old men are better lovers than young men."

This tendency to embody what he saw or heard around him as something immediately affecting him touched on other physical matters. Once, walking in Bal Harbour, we heard a distant explosion. People in the shopping mall turned slowly, no great shock in the far-away sound, but Singer walking at my side waited a few seconds—well into a time when he knew he was safe—and then threw himself to the ground. I helped him up, and asked, "What are you doing?"

He said, "Well, you never know."

"For God's sakes, you knew that sound was fifty miles away. Nothing's going to get you and even if it does it's better to just go than it is to jump at sounds and shadows."

He smiled his best. "You know I'm not an American," he said. "I'm not like you. When something happens in Poland everyone runs around and screams. If it was a Polish bus and it hit a bump there'd be screaming, tearing hair: 'Why is this happening? Where's my Mendel?' On an airplane here, you know, the plane jumps, it bumps, there is low conversation, quiet, it's a difference in America. Hysteria there, everything is hysteria."

The histrionic quality of his fictions and perhaps even certain character traits could be explained by what he regarded as European hysteria. But there was a large personal, competitive area in Singer's psyche, and it was barely beneath the surface, at least with me.

Walking one day on Harding toward Bal Harbour, the two of us quiet, I waited for him to talk. In his solemn moods I did not try to provoke conversation. A conversation with Isaac, when it was serious, was not simply direct candor but bursts of the plainest language possible on his part. He seldom used profanity: I heard him curse only three times in ten years. Once, when we were alone, he said—in Yiddish—as we spoke of a woman who had had him moments ago sign a petition regarding the status of Yiddish at the university, "She can kiss a monkey's ass!" He said it in exasperation with her pursuit of him and his inability to refuse her. The other two times were when he used, laughing heartily, the Yiddish word *couter*, which he said means "to have sexual intercourse." He asked, red-faced and pleased, "Did President Kennedy couter her?" and another time, speaking of a former and legendary dean, said, "So he couters, he couters the woman." His descriptions of metaphysical insights, or worldly knowledge, were also spoken in plain terms: "I'll tell you, my friend," he started off; and then, "All women are crazy, they do not make sense even to themselves"; or, "Let me explain this to you: children must never be given a penny by their fathers, not a penny."

Walking with him, I observed a small, fat boy running in an awkward side-to-side waddle. About eleven, the kid ran across Harding and then stopped, breathing hard. I said to Isaac, breaking our silence, "Isn't it peculiar, ungainly people who have no special physical abilities do the same things athletes do? They don't see themselves."

"What? What?"

"That little boy," I said, "he's so fat he can hardly walk and still he loves to run. He thinks he's running like an athlete."

"What?" Singer asked, and I could see he was angry and that "Polish hysteria" or self-involvement had joined us on the sidewalk.

"The boy!" I said. "He's running, he's funny, the little fat boy."

Singer bent his head, turned from me, and ran up Harding away from me, ran and ran. Ran head down, arms stiff at his sides, legs churning up to the corner of Harding. He stopped and waited for me to catch up.

Looking directly into my eyes, he said, "I can run."

Afterward, on days when he sprinted across the street as we crossed at a light, I said to him, "You can make my basketball team any time," and he laughed each time as if he'd heard it that day for the first time.

Another story in class by a female student amazed him into silence. Quietly, in a well-modulated voice, a young woman read a story about a man and a woman, strangers, who lived across from each other in an apartment complex, but they could see each other over their balconies. They stood out in the early evening and Sunday mornings and fulfilled themselves by masturbating for their own and the other's amusement. After class—it was one of the days I drove Singer home—he asked, "Tell me, what were they doing out there at the windows? I didn't hear her."

"Masturbating."

"Masturbating? Who? What?"

"Playing with themselves."

He fell into a deep silence, and I couldn't restrain myself. I burst into laughter. But he wouldn't be tempted into a discussion of the story. He sat in silence and jumped from the car at the Surfside Towers. "Goodbye," he said, and walked away quickly, avoiding contagion.

Criticized for sexual obsessions, Singer often took narrow positions that would have surprised critics of his alleged libertine fancies. "He's the worst homophobe in the world," a tall man, late twenties, leather-jacketed, said to me after an intersession class. He was an unregistered visitor. It was not our regular class but a workshop I conducted between semesters, and Singer graciously came often, giving the work-a-day quality of the proceedings, sometimes a meat-and-potatoes branch of adult education, a glamour it otherwise lacked.

The tall man was mean. He leaned into me. "You'd like it, wouldn't you, if all the homosexuals got gassed the way the Jews did, wouldn't you? Your buddy there would."

I twisted away from him. "I have no quarrel with homosexuals," I said brilliantly.

"Your pal does," he said, and spat.

On another occasion our class was attended by two visiting Chinese mainland scholars. They sat enthralled for what was from my point of view a very bad session indeed. One of the stories under consideration struck on all of Isaac's taboos: he did not care for stories about Jews or Jewish families; he did not enjoy stories with profanity in them (one young woman wrote a story with last-exit-to-Brooklyn profanity, and when I asked her why, knowing this wasn't her idiom, she said, "To make Singer mad"). The Jewish family story was about a tough-talking young woman looking for a husband and her hard-swearing, grammatically inept family that fractured English. The young woman in the story used profanity and apparently had a great many lovers, and Isaac Singer liked nothing about it. He worked into his tirade about a lack of uniqueness his observation that the story was vulgar. I found it had vital dialogue, a good sense of narrative, and interesting, if familiar, characters. I said nothing about profanity. The student seemed pleased at my response.

Singer said, "A good writer shouldn't use profanity."

I asked, "Why?"

Singer said, "It's vulgar and people don't like to read it."

"What people?" I asked. "After all, it's Sandra's story and she writes it the way she wants to and maybe there are people who won't mind the profanity. Maybe she's not even writing it for publication."

"No good writer uses bad language," he said, and the two Chinese scholars nodded their heads.

"Gentlemen," I asked, "are there rules against writing profanity in fiction in China?"

"There are no rules," one said, "but we do not have the kind of writers who write this kind of language."

"Do ordinary people in China curse?" I asked.

"Yes," he said, "but our writers do not put it into their fiction."

An older woman in the class—to remind the Chinese scholars where they were—said, "I resent you two," meaning Singer and me, "getting up there and commenting on a woman's story. A man can't possibly understand a woman like the woman in the story."

I turned to the student whose story it was and asked, "Do you think I understand your story?"

She turned back to the older woman with some anger and said, "Professor Goran understands my story. I like what he said."

"It burns me up," the older woman said.

I turned to the class and said, "I get combat pay for these sessions." And I said to the visitors, "I think in our country it's assumed that thirty centuries' struggle behind us have earned us the right to use any kind of language appropriate to our thoughts in fiction. It may be vulgar or foolish or inept, but it's a right we take for granted."

They were amiable and I was friendly and we all smiled. I asked the class if they'd like to ask our visitors some questions and if the scholars cared to answer. They were agreeable, and the class asked about life and students in China (this was 1986) and we were all filled with international goodwill. At the end I said I'd like to live in China, and one of the scholars said, "We'd like to have you." And I said, "I won't allow cursing around me, I promise."

At the end of the semester, as the students formed a small line to get Singer's autograph or to say goodbye, the older woman, quite tall, shouted to me over the heads of the other students in a jovial tone, "He's the worst male chauvinist in the world!" Meaning Singer.

Singer, the writer, knew my feelings well as each semester closed. He described all the class terms Isaac and I served together. He wrote in "The Bus," " 'Don't rush,' she said. 'Unlike the driver of our ill-starred bus, the forces that drive us mad have all the time in the world.' "

Notwithstanding the justifiable pleasure he received from the marvelous stories he and I worked on weekly in the game room, I sensed in Singer a restlessness, even unhappiness, in the fall of 1983. He had watched me more closely than ever when we taught together that spring, and he had argued with me about subjects in my own writing—as if what I did mattered. These were bad signs, omens I took for a lack of confidence in himself. The Singer of disdain and imperial distance was my old pal. The Isaac Singer who had boarded a train for Warsaw, leaving his parents with no regrets—and, he told me, never looking back or wanting to see them again—was not one who thrived on literary indecision. All the creeps and lurches were reserved for sidewalks and rooms, not for the pure desires of his writing. He fudged about his writing, of course, altered his biography for interviews to suit nuances of his spirit at the moment, told dramatic tales about it, and invented crisis and dilemma; but his writing stayed—despite his frequent, modest "Not bad for a scribbler,

huh?"—a rock in the center of his perplexity. That fall he stiffened
and became as angrily positive in manner as he had been in the great
days of altering his will. Singer in a mode of certainty was possessed.
It was the refuge he took when he was frightened.

He had concluded that he did not like Paul Kresh's biography, *The
Magician of West Eighty-Sixth Street*. Kresh had quoted Irving Howe,
one of Singer's first and most eloquent explicators. Howe had said in
1977 Singer was slowing down. Another anecdote in the book, told
by Cecil Helmly's wife, suggested that Singer had worn out Cecil
Helmly, one of his early translators, and had shown little regard for
his early efforts on Isaac's behalf. (To me he seemed sad about Helmly
and spoke of his translator's self-destructive habits, never of his
uncounted contributions to the Singer career.) Also, there was
another anecdote by Mrs. Helmly, who spoke of a pompous speech
Isaac made on taking a frog away from a child and throwing it back
into a pool, hurting the child but making his point.

I do not know what else bothered him about the Kresh book. At
first he liked it; then, I'm sure, either Alma read him selected parts
or someone warned him about it. From then Kresh was almost a taboo
subject. (Also taboo was Howe, whose fine work on Singer and other
subjects I mentioned often at the beginning with Isaac, thinking I was
on safe ground, only to be met with grim withdrawal. I continued to
read Howe in secret.)

When I boldly asked one day in 1983 about Paul Kresh, I saw the
depth of Isaac's feelings.

"I don't want to see his face," he said. "Schmearer. Do you know
what a schmearer is?"

"Yes."

"You know what a schmearer is?"

"Yes, I do."

"How do you know this?"

"Isaac, I told you I spoke Yiddish before I spoke English. My
mother spoke Yiddish, my father spoke Yiddish, the neighbors spoke
Yiddish. I speak Yiddish now and I understand Yiddish now."

"So you know what's a schmearer?"

"Yes, a flatterer."

He turned to me with pleasure. "Ah, you do know what a schmearer is!"

"You mean Kresh flatters aimlessly?"

"He has no character," Singer said. "I forbid him to come to my apartment. I'll slam the door in his face."

On another occasion the subject of Kresh's book came up while Alma, Isaac, and I were having breakfast, and Alma interrupted something I was saying and said, "He [Kresh] writes about things he shouldn't write about."

"Agh!" Isaac said, sawing the air in dismissal.

"You mean personal things?" I asked.

"No, not personal things," she said—and I took that to mean not sexual things about Isaac—"just things nobody wants to know about."

"Like what?"

"He's a schmearer," Isaac said, "that's it."

"Does Lester know what that means?" Alma asked.

The subject in my book Mrs. *Beautiful* that bothered him was a strike that occurred in 1908. No matter how I argued with him that labor unrest was an important part of American history and that the strike in my book, while one of the most dramatic of the century, was anything but central to the theme of Mrs. *Beautiful*, he insisted, "You cannot write about a strike!"

"Yes, I can. I can write about anything I want."

"You want to get published. Who would publish a book about a strike?"

"It's not a book about a strike."

"If a strike is in it it's a book about a strike. A leftist book."

"You know I'm not a leftist."

"So why do you write a leftist book? It won't get published."

"I don't care if it doesn't get published if someone thinks it's about a strike," I said. "It's about a woman who makes magical corsets."

He brightened. "So leave out the strike," he said, and then, "A writer shouldn't write a book that doesn't get published."

"I'm not disagreeing with you," I said, "I'm just telling you a book that has a strike in it can get published."

"Jews always write books about strikes."

"So, I'm a Jew," I said. "But there aren't any Jews in my novel."

"No Jews?"

"God, Isaac, there's a whole radical movement in the United States that had a native background mostly without Jews." I gave him a short bustling history of the International Workers of the World, the Amalgamated Iron and Tin Workers, their enemies, the Pinkerton Detective Agency. "I'd like to do a book on Alan Pinkerton, the founder, someday—and the lives of people touched by labor unrest."

He was not unmoved, but he said, "The communists took them over."

"I think so," I said.

"They were all dupes of the communists."

"This is a conversation for another day."

He watched me carefully now through slow, appraising blue eyes. "You know, my friend," he said, "I am going to publish a radical book." He laughed. "So am I still a bourgeois?" he asked.

He called me a "hawk" because I followed military campaigns all over the world. He regarded me as a "sentimentalist" because I favored Israel in its conflicts with the Arabs. He said I was "avant-garde" because I liked writers like Bellow(!) and even found Barthelme funny (and alternately he said I was "kitsch" because I read the sports news in the paper).

I had called him a name only once. In early exasperation with his sexual attitudes generally, I said, "You're a bourgeois, Isaac, and try to hide it," and I never heard the end of it. I might as well have called him a Yiddishist, so keenly did he feel the defamation.

"What's your radical book called?" I asked.

He reveled now in that peculiar certainty, laughing long and sure. "*The Penitent*," he said. "My publishers say not to publish it, but we will see. Now, do you see how bold I can be?"

"Well, you're old enough to know what you're doing. But why don't they want to publish it?"

He said angrily, "Because it's the truth."

Later that day he told me, "It's my story." And at another time he said, "It's my whole philosophy." Still later, he said, "It's my most important book."

Kresh describes in his book, written before *The Penitent* was published in the United States, that Singer's "literary advisers" discouraged him from publishing the book. That part of his life was unknown to me, so I do not know who it was that had warned him; but they were right. The novel is an ill-conceived polemic, making sense neither as a statement of religious belief (equating Judaism with a sort of desert captivity of docile women and children by righteous men) nor as a work of fiction with its obsessive voice of the would-be prophet dominating and suffocating the story.

The distance between Isaac Singer, presumably the man who starts out telling the story, and the actual narrator in *The Penitent* is as narrow as such things can be. For once it is not possible to accept a narrator in Singer as merely an artful fictional tool. Joseph Shapiro, whose tale it is, has read everything of the author's, quotes his work, has heard him speak often, holds easily identifiable opinions of Singer's, and in the book comments on the remarkable coincidences between the lives of the two of them: he is from a rabbinical family like Singer's. It's clear that this is a book in which character and the clash of personalities are not Singer's main interest. It is a philosophical argument ineptly composed as fiction.

The narrator, Shapiro, is a man seeking to justify a thesis held by Singer: the modern world has gone to hell. America, Israel, the rest. The usually balanced voices in Singer—few villains, few heroes, the customary temperaments and sensibilities contending for our interest—vanish under the rage of the author's antagonisms. He is not just dark about modern times; he is bleak and ridiculous. He is not pessimistic and jolly with Singer's quick wink at the absurdity even of his pessimism; he is in a fog of misapprehensions.

Singer, despite a feeble disclaimer in the book—too blithely stated—that he is not Shapiro, is obviously endorsing Joseph Shapiro's rejection of the contemporary world. Otherwise why take time to outline at some length the visions of a crackpot? Written in "the early seventies" according to Kresh (dated by David Neal Miller in *Fear of Fiction* as published in 1971 in Tel Aviv), it is Singer's frightened response to the years of social and political turmoil of the sixties. He still maintained these dreads in 1983 when I knew him and when the book was published in the U.S.

Reading it, one finds a vision of reality that Singer holds along with his geniality. Having told me with passion that this is his story and the truth, I think *The Penitent's* darkness and wrath is a side of him that can't be ignored. It is not all of him, of course, not his rich talent for wit and narrative, but it was the side often visible to me, as he felt suffocated by modernity.

Coming to class in January 1984, resolute and troubled, Singer had read that fall the reviews of this novel he considered important, and our conspiracy began to crack. Only a person hopelessly out of tune with the dissonant life and the frustrations of creating reality out of language will fail to understand Isaac Singer's chagrin. Alternating between his peculiar bravado and stark uncertainty he marched into our class in 1984 for what proved to be the beginning of the long end of his career as a visiting Monday-afternoon prophet.

In the *New York Times Book Review* in September 1983, Harold Bloom wrote that the title of the book meant literally "The Master of Turning" and said quite directly that this book "ought not to have been published at all." He said that it is "a very unpleasant work, without a redeeming esthetic merit or humane quality," and that Singer's best book was his *Collected Stories* (1982). He called *The Penitent* a "failed attempt at a Swiftian diatribe against the contemporary world" and "his worst book"; he found that it "sadly defines much that is uneasy and probably insolvable in the dilemma of Jewish culture at this time."

Bloom found Singer's strength to be not in polemics but in a "raw experience of narrative rather than in the creation of character." Singer's voice in the novel, he said, was "negative, intense, apprehensive, fascinated by lust yet filled with revulsion towards it. The voice is indistinguishable from Singer's own and there is no way to read this book except as Singer's tirade." He compared the long speech to "a kind of monologue that in Bellow would be deliberately satirical," adding that Singer's "musings in defense of creationism" are "worthy to be taken up by the Rev. Jerry Falwell." Bloom found Singer more interested in interpretations than in the Scriptures. "The basement of a house is not as elegant as a drawing room," he quoted Singer, suggesting that "traditional Jewish interpreters are too tame for the ethos of Singer's world."

"Singer/Shapiro," Bloom wrote, "is thus . . . in agreement with Freud, though he does not know it." He then cited various incidents in the book as having an "involuntary humor," mentioning an improbable sex scene aboard an airplane.

Bloom asked the question "How has Singer come down to this?" and finds—in my view a highly debatable thesis—that Freud and Kafka are "the authentic representations of Jewish culture in and of our time," dismissing Singer's novel as "Jewish literary neo-orthodoxy." He then concluded, "Had Singer written often thus he would indeed be remembered as a master of neo-orthodoxy, but hardly a master of the intricate turnings of the stories."

There was for Singer no comfort elsewhere in book reviews that fall. In September *Newsweek* placed him third in their book section, after two books by Latin American writers in an omnibus review and a book about children in war-torn countries. His reviewer, Peter S. Prescott, who had been particularly eloquent in his appreciations of Singer when he received the Nobel Prize in 1978, wrote, "Surely this novel will shock many of Isaac Bashevis Singer's devoted readers. . . . Didactic in form, it bears a dismal message that directly contradicts the humor, the complexity, the sensual joy of living that so many of his stories so delightfully convey. The passionate obsessiveness which has in the past undone so many of Singer's characters is now shown to be the only path to redemption . . . not through joy, through anger."

In *Time* that October, Singer was placed after *The Collected Stories of Bernard Malamud* in the book section and was reviewed together with a book about Isaac and his brother by Clive Sinclair, *The Brothers Singer*. "Shapiro is afflicted with a temperament suited less to a religious zealot than a retrograde cab driver," the reviewer wrote. And once more the phrase "no redeeming features" was used to describe elements in the novel.

The fall of 1983 had seemed to prove Isaac wrong. Bloom's question "How has Singer come down to this?" hovered about my friend as he made his way to English 560 in the spring of 1984. Without examining the queer convolutions in the novel, noted earlier in the Victorian guesswork about eyes, it is enough to say that something important to Singer had failed. He had too ferociously revealed himself after a lifetime of concealment. The young woman Shapiro marries, she of the Judaism about the eyes, is quiet as a mouse, obedient, and—God help all men in their dream of lost virgins— twenty-four years old, but looks eighteen.

He was eighty in 1984 and both shaken and confident as he sat down at our long conference table and, leaning back, said, "Ladies, there are no rules. This is the only rule."

✑ Chapter Five

SINGER'S CONCERNS DID did not diminish the pleasures in our long Sundays that year. *The Penitent* and its discontents must have seemed far away to him on a balmy autumn Sunday as we walked down Harding and around the Bal Harbour Shops and then, the day being so rare, out Collins to sit on a bench and watch traffic and the people across the street at the mall.

The bench was shady. Isaac asked me if I had a mortgage on my house, and I said I did. He said he was afraid of investing in any kind of real estate, even his condominium.

"It's as easy as signing one piece of paper as another," I said. "Do you think if you bought an apartment house you'd have to change the light bulbs yourself?"

He laughed, and I asked, "Do you think you'd have to go out and sweep the driveway or front hall?"

"No," he said, "but I'd identify myself too much with the tenants. Once, I lived in an apartment rented to me by a landlord who lived there too, a man named Zapritsky, and when it rained or the weather was bad Zapritsky's tenants would call and complain to me. I agreed with all of them on the telephone. When they'd call to tell me the roof was leaking, I'd say, 'My god! that's terrible.' I could never be a landlord. I think too much like the tenants."

"I never heard you talk about Zapritsky," I said.

"This Zapritsky," Singer said, "was a big, fat man. He had a stomach that went out to that curb." Singer pointed to the curb ten feet away. "I asked myself—since all Jews are supposed to be brothers—what do I have in common with this man?" He wrinkled up his face. "And I decided," he said, "I'll choose my own brothers."

84

"So you don't want to be a big, fat man," I said, "like Zapritsky. That's why you're not a landlord."

"They tear up the houses, the tenants," he said.

"What tenants?"

"The blacks."

"I lived in a government housing project," I said. "Black and white. The manager was a black named Shelton. When he was there nobody tore up anything. He'd throw them out."

"The blacks can't help themselves," Singer said, "they're physical."

He made a gesture with his arms, standing up and making fists at his sides. "When they walk down the steps"—he made walking movements with his feet, bouncing along—"they break the steps." He sat down again. "When they open doors"—he made a move toward a doorknob as he sat—"they pull out the frame. They're very strong."

"Come on, Isaac, you see weak black people all the time on the street."

He laughed. "They wouldn't live in my house. I'd have strong ones. My house would be a wreck in a week. They break the steps the way they walk."

The first week of class he told me he did not want to ride to the university anymore with the young woman who had volunteered to drive him. He called me after class and said that she drives "side to side. No more."

"She's an honors student."

"She has accidents, she told me. No more! You drive me."

"I can't. I have a class in the morning on Mondays."

"She drives side to side."

The new chairman of English, John Paul Russo, had reassured me early on that he thought Isaac Singer was one of the great writers of his time and he would do anything he could to make Singer happy. I went to him with my own concerns.

"I don't want to do this anymore, John Paul," I said.

Russo was working on his biography of I. A. Richards, having already spent eight years of the twelve it would take him to complete it. He had known Richards at Harvard, knew him well, and lived in his home in England when he traveled there. What I told him about my problems and wanting to quit teaching a class with Isaac Singer struck a responsive chord.

"Do you think he'll work with Anna [not her name]?" he asked, naming a female colleague.

"No, it's out of the question."

"How about Bruce?" and he named a grad student.

"It would last two weeks," I said. "Do you want to lose him?"

"I don't want to lose him," Russo said, "but I have a responsibility to you, too."

"I'm glad you're sympathetic," I said. "I'm going to call on you as soon as I figure something out."

"I want to keep him," he said, "but I want to be fair too."

The whirlwind around Isaac, after *The Penitent,* now settled on transportation. His rides to and from the university in those ten years were two-thirds of the problems in my life. He was never pleased.

The female student who voluntarily drove him often in 1983 and 1982 had told him in passing that she had been in an accident once. "An accident means it wasn't her fault," I pleaded with him that week. "She's reliable and careful. She's an honors student. The accident happened six years ago. She loves you, Isaac. She's been doing a great job for two years."

"She drives from side to side," he said, and that was the end of it.

I used to let people into our highly selective writing class because they promised to chauffeur him, lived on Miami Beach, or planned to do a dissertation on him some day and *welcomed* driving him. One woman quit driving in the second week, having been accepted into the class. She smiled at me all semester with sweet superiority as I wrestled each week to put together a list of drivers to bring and take him. A woman who once offered us tickets to a golf tournament(!) had, Singer told me, talked so much that he said to her, "It's not necessary, my dear woman, to tell everyone everything that's on your mind." To me, he said, "If she drives me one more time I will jump from the car!" For years I sat by the telephone in my office on

Monday mornings waiting for calls from students, Alma Singer, or taxicab drivers. Deedee sat home waiting for the same calls. He was late, he was early, the student was lost. Our youngest son, John, stood at the ready to dash off and rescue him on the highway for the future of student fiction writing.

On a morning in February, sunny as Miami can be on its brightest spring day, I went out to wait for Isaac and his cab at the fountain near the Ashe Building with my friend, former student, and colleague novelist Kathleen Martell Gordon. A pale brunette who taught courses in creative writing at the university, she is relative to this morning in February, in excellent physical condition, running miles almost every day. She is wearing a coral-colored dress and high heels. She is laughing and talking while we wait. At the time I have known her about twelve years.

He was late. I asked Kathleen to wait at the fountain while I ran up the stairs to see if there were any messages. There was one from Deedee. Alma had called to say that Isaac was sick but coming. I ran back downstairs.

After about ten minutes, a taxicab appeared with a Haitian driver. He quickly rounded the fountain circle—Singer was three quarters of an hour late—and began his departure toward the main gate, still with Isaac in the cab.

"Wait!" I shouted, and the driver stopped, and in a flash, about twenty feet away from us, Singer leaped out and began running in the opposite direction away from Kathleen and me.

Kathleen, who thinks I am stiff in public, asked, "Do you want me to chase him?"

"God, yes!"

She jumped on a stone bench in her path, jumped off, and ran full tilt in her high heels across a lawn. He was no match in a race with her. She caught him before he had run fifty feet into the main road.

I said to the cab driver, "What's the matter with you?"

He said, laughing, "That old man's crazy. He don't know where he's going. He tell me one thing, then he tell another, then he say, 'Take me home!'"

Singer was shouting at me as Kathleen led him toward me, "Where's the President? I want to resign. Where's the President?"

Now, remarkably at that moment, President Tad Foote, who is a tall, easily observed figure, walked by Singer, Kathleen, and me.

"Ah," Singer said, "there he is. I want to resign."

Lost in thought, President Foote, a fast walker, did not see our tableau and kept walking briskly toward the Ashe Building.

"President!" Isaac said, moving toward him, but I took Isaac's arm.

"This is no place to do this," I said, appealing to his sense of decorum, and he slowed down. My feeling of love for him returned in a large, overwhelming wave: he was bleeding at the bridge of his nose where his glasses had pushed against his face. He was alternately pale and flushed, feverish. He was a lamb frightened before wolves. I put my arm around his shoulder and thanked Kathleen, who was close to tears.

Composing himself, he said to her, "Are you a college professor?"

She said, "Yes."

He said, "I thought all college professors had beards."

I led Isaac to a men's room where he washed and cooled himself.

I called Alma, and she said, "He's like a madman, with a fever. He said he'd lose his job if he didn't go today. He bumped his nose; he's bleeding. He said you will fire him." I reassured her, saying he was fine for the moment.

Knowing what I said would make no impression at all, I said to him, "You don't have to come out here when you're sick."

He said, "I must come. My students are waiting."

While the class was in session, I went in a rage to my chairman, and said, "John Paul, another cab driver got lost, I can't get a student to drive him—he hates them all—and I'm not making two trips to Surfside every Monday." I suppose I hoped John Paul would say, "Well, this is the end then," sharing with me the onus of losing Isaac Bashevis Singer to the university.

Instead Russo said, "We'll hire a limousine and pick him up at home Mondays, have the limo wait during class, and take him home after class. Is that all right with you?"

The white stretch limousine cost two hundred dollars a Monday. At first, the limousine came too early or too late to pick him up in Surfside; then a driver could not find the University of Miami; and occasionally the limo, too, was stalled in traffic.

The long, white limo in time became Isaac to us and to others at the school. I waited by the fountain for it to arrive, the friendly drivers to help him out, the precious moment when I could put him safely back into the red plush seats and see him depart for another Monday. At the Surfside Towers, where daily plans were made for trips to Gulfstream Race Track by bus—with shouts across the lobby about Dave's goiter and where was Phil (heard while I transcribed masterworks by a genius at a small table in the game room while people entered or left)—one could only imagine the excitement as the limo arrived and the man among them who had made it got aboard.

Alma, on departure from Surfside in the limousine, stopped a moment at its door, savoring her exit; but Isaac, being himself, hurtled past her and threw himself into the seats or shoved her, and, as best she could, she took her place. Alighting at the university, there was about Alma the sense of a visitor to a foreign country, composed (ah, here are the natives), while Singer stepped out and immediately began to spin in a circle in his anxiety to get started in some direction. As to her coming to class, he invented for her the fiction that I had ordered her never to appear, and, despite my protests to the contrary, she insisted that I did not want her. It was not true.

Alma Singer, for all her dubious claims to aristocracy, was an intelligent, well-read woman who understood her husband's writing as well as anyone short of one who had made a professional career of it. She knew where he was at his best and often directed me to something in his work I'd missed, and invariably she was accurate. She and I shared the same enthusiasms for things Isaac had created. She knew good from bad about writing generally, and, while she absorbed Isaac's prejudices, she was a woman of taste—I found her often so in clothes and food and decor—and she was bound to an aesthetic anarchist. At his best, he went along with her sound judgments about life and art; at his worst he tolerated her.

Where she came apart was in her grandiose dreams about herself and her past. She was just fine. She was not nobility, and, arriving at the university, the woman who had told a *Miami Herald* feature writer that she'd given up her career as a writer when she married Isaac asserted herself. She commented on the fiction being read in class, often at my request (could I ignore her?), with a vehemence and clicking of her tongue and rolling of her head that indicated disagreement with almost anything else that was said. Not that she didn't have insights into what was being discussed; she was good at it, but she was intemperate, swinging about to look at what sounded like an argument with her and making a disapproving sound.

She also wanted to sit in the front of the classroom, as if she, Isaac, and I were a trio there to be honored at a luncheon or a group of authors being interviewed at a forum. And when I told her I thought it best she sit in a special seat (with someone I chose for the moment for her to meet), Isaac's claim that I didn't want her took shape. I sincerely invited her to come ten times a year, perhaps a hundred and fifty times in the ten years I worked with Isaac Singer, and she never failed to say to me—even when she accepted—"Isaac says you don't want me."

He announced to the class one week in the conference room, where reminders of need and age spoke to Singer in every syllable he heard, that women are more sensitive than men.

Tere Trout, in medical school when I last heard from her, said, "Yes, they have periods every month."

Like a good athletic coach, Singer knew when not to hear one of his surly players. He immediately stopped praising women, knowing he was somehow off in his catering and some women in class were hearing something he hoped he wasn't saying. Distracted as he was that spring, nothing was working well.

One week, while a white woman declaimed a story in what she thought was a black dialect, complete with "Hit him upside the head!" Singer leaped up at the table and searched himself. He had been given a medal as the class began by a student organization. It was fastened to a ribbon and had been placed around his neck; he had put it in his coat pocket. And while the woman dramatized her story by shouting platitudes of pseudo-black street talk, Singer shouted over her, "Where's my medal?"

Everything stopped as the class looked about in guilty apprehension. "Where's Dr. Goran?" he shouted.

I was down the corridor in my office. I had read the story that morning and was weary of the black talk and dramatic reading. I came running at Singer's cries. He was already in the corridor, searching himself and repeatedly calling my name. As calm descended, he found the medal, the woman continued, and I walked back down to my office with her voice ringing in the halls. I watched the shadows in the spiky, flat leaves of the sapodilla tree outside my window.

When she was through Singer asked, "Are there black people in this story?"

The student explained her life up to that point in great detail. Isaac listened. The rest of us waited for limousine time.

It was the next week that the doubt about the publication of *The Penitent*, like the red death, crept into our small conference room on the third floor of Ashe. The trip out to the university had gone well, the day was bountiful with promise, and the story that Monday was by a good writer, John Oudens. Oudens, clear in thought, read well and loudly, and his story, "Angel Wings," was interesting. In it a boy of about eleven lies in the snow on his back and makes circular motions and leaves indentations in the snow, designs that children call angel wings. I'd never done that up north when I was a child, but some of the students in the class had. When the boy in the story comes back some years later to where he had made the wings in the snow, he discovers out in the woods the lovely crypt of a young girl he had once loved. The story was simple, direct, and had no literary allusions. There were no disjunctive sequences in time; the vocabulary was nothing to startle Bilgoray's most eminent citizen; there was no profanity, and no crude jests were made at the expense of the sexuality of elderly men.

Singer, for a reason still unknown to me, opened in a burst with his most vituperative epithet the minute Oudens was through: "This is an *experimental* story!" The word to Isaac was synonymous with ungodly. "It is—what they call *avant-garde*," he said, evoking his quarrel with Bohemians or the displacement of Russian peasants in 1933.

The distinction between the years when communism could represent expressions in poetry and fiction as varied as symbolism or surrealism and the grim later period, after Mayakovsky and Mandelstam (and Babel, who fit nowhere except in the land and times of the original genius), of Soviet Realism, with odes to tractors and irrigated fields, was lost on Singer. What he meant by "experimental" was simply fancy English locutions or vocabulary or events arranged in nonchronological sequences. When he could follow the story somewhat but was still confused and when it had enough details of place, Singer called it "a slice of life," somewhat attaching his own meaning to the genre. But we were somewhere else with him: he could not imagine the configuration of design in the snow put there by the boy in the story. Students stood and showed him, no one lying down on the floor, and I drew it on the board. No, he said, this story made no sense, and he refused to say more.

I reassured Oudens—and so did others—that we liked the story and the matter was seemingly put away with all the rest of what had passed on another Monday afternoon. But walking to the limo, Singer asked me for a copy of the story, rather good-naturedly, and I gave it to him, and we bid each other farewell.

He called me an hour later, and in an anguished voice, said, "I do not understand this story. I will resign. I should not be teaching students. This is a story that makes no sense. What is it 'Angel Wings'?"

Again, I explained, and again he said, "I will resign" before he hung up.

The day was growling at my heels. Why was this story chosen as the words of the apocalypse? I decided it was more Isaac than the class or the story.

He called me again about nine that night. "Alma is home now," he said, "and she will read the story and she will tell us whether it makes sense."

"Good," I said. "But, Isaac, if Alma says it doesn't make sense that won't change my opinion. I think it's a good story."

"We will see," he said, and then, "I should not be teaching at the university."

The next day he called me at the university and asked, "Can you come down this week?"

"Sunday," I said. "I was planning on breakfast, same as always."

"I must see you sooner," he said. "I am in distress."

"About what?"

"Alma says the story makes sense."

"Isaac, we all have opinions. Our opinions differ, that's all."

"No, I am a fraud."

"Now you're talking crazy."

"The story has no beginning and no end. What are angel wings?"

"I'll tell you when I see you."

"Please, come sooner."

I came somewhat uneasily on Thursday morning and had a literary conference with Alma and Isaac. He was genuinely stricken at his failure to grasp this story—forgetting the forty others he had condemned on grounds no more solid—and I reassured him that I understood his confusion. I invented places and language in the story that were obscure, unclear, and ambiguous and Alma agreed, and after an hour we persuaded Isaac not to resign.

On our walk after breakfast, he said, "You know I understood that story made no sense. Now you showed me. It was a trick, right? The story was a kind of joke."

I did not want him to withdraw in defeat. I wanted him to be academically judicious, balanced in tone, analytic with an open mind to others' sensibilities: to be respectful of fictions other than his own and to take the America around him and its youth we were charged to teach on somewhat more of its and their own terms. I asked of him only that he not be Isaac Bashevis Singer.

We paved it over by forgetting about the subject (until he brought it up once or twice outside of class as an example of "phony" experimental fiction, and then I told him that Oudens had received a fellowship in creative writing from the University of New Hampshire, and he never mentioned the story again).

That Sunday as we walked after breakfast, he took my arm, stopping me as we walked, a signal to the urgency of his report. "Every day I see more and more the hand of God. I know for sure now."

Isaac and Alma Singer lived on the ninth floor of a condominium building. From their sunny and airy condominium at 9511 Collins Avenue (for which he'd paid $76,000 and insisted—against all logic at the astronomical price increases in housing around him—he would lose it all), Singer could encompass all his needs within a span of twenty minutes: daily to the drugstore for breakfast; next door to Danny's for lunch or dinner; a walk through the Bal Harbour Shops ten minutes away, where he never once in the ten years we strolled there looked into a store window. There was a public library and a physician arranged for his service under rather dramatic circumstances on Isaac Singer Road all lying reassuringly at hand. No ordinary need ever broke in on him or interrupted his reveries. He experienced little that might startle him into immediacy.

I envied his intactness and dreaded the isolation he carried around with him like an ambulatory patient with a self-contained oxygen tent.

"You know those students in class, the geniuses?" he asked. I knew the two he meant. They were reasonably, if generically, articulate graduate students. "There were writers like that in Warsaw."

"One of the geniuses in our class could be a writer, the other never."

"In Warsaw none of them were writers," he said. "Those geniuses, how is it they can talk so well about writing and they write so poorly?"

"The classroom is everything to some English graduate students," I said. "It's what they're doing. School, class. They're not learning to be writers; they're going to school, and what they do is talk well about writing in class. The classroom, talking about writing, is all there is for them."

"I never heard such talk, honestly."

"They're good at it."

"They know what's wrong with everybody's story," he said, "but they can't write a story on their own."

I felt at that time on Collins, on a particularly long walk out past the Bal Harbour Shops, an affinity I always had for him when we talked about writing and he spoke in his truest voice. We worked on his stories, and I was alternately thrilled to be in his company, bored with the repetitiousness of the process of transcribing, amused at his breakfast wit, and devoted to the brave man he was with it all: a writer, Isaac Bashevis Singer, one of a kind, lamblike in humility in part, lionlike in his vision of the writer's role (survive, then attack), kind and selfish and complex beyond the capacity of language to capture whatever there was in the man that was the basis for the artist. Or was it the other way around?

The pleasure in working with me was perhaps that I was so easy. His heart's delight was not to pay me for anything. Of the stories I worked on with him in *The Death of Methuselah* (1988), I received nothing for the six with my name attached. I never questioned him about it. I pretended ignorance. I made it easy, and probably—who knows?—that's why Isaac Singer occasionally loved me. He sensed in me, gifted man that he was, the fool beneath the college professor. One too dumb to know he'd been swindled, the son of the sort of people he had seen in Bialystok, my mother's country village in Poland, and he wondered about their intelligence, not being one of them. Now he knew for sure.

I goaded him about a small coincidence in return for his lack of respect for my ancestral wit. My Yiddish name is Itche, the same derivation as Isaac, or Yitzchak. So we're both Yitzchak. And, oddly, my mother's name was Silverman, and his mother's name was Zylberman. We are both named Yitzchak Silberman, I reminded him with malicious relish from time to time.

After one of his successful speeches on the campus, a good number of the six hundred people in Gusman Hall rushed down to mill about him and I observed a middle-aged woman hovering near, about twenty feet from him, not trying to talk to him.

I said to her, "You can talk to him. Don't be shy."

She said, "Oh, no."

I asked, "What are you doing?"

"I'm standing in his aura; I want to stand in his aura," she said.

When people asked if they could attend class as one-day visitors, they often said, "I just want to be in the same room with him." In New York he attracted on the streets and in restaurants people shamelessly saying his name to each other and standing at their booths and tables to observe him better. In Miami and New York people walked up to his table to talk to him, usually about somewhere they'd heard him talk, not as often about reading something of his. "Gimpel the Fool" was the work mentioned most frequently when they spoke of his writing. Street scenes with him were as singular as one of his stories.

One late twilight he and I were walking down West End Avenue down from his apartment on West 86th Street. It was a lovely night, the streets lit by the sun falling over the buildings and evening shadows still an hour away. We'd walked and sat on benches on the west side of Central Park, commented on things around us, and stood and walked again, sat, had dinner, and strolled down West End Avenue. He did not want to break off the talk. He promised he'd take a cab back to his apartment as we headed toward Central Park South where I was staying. It was a warm night in June. A man standing in a doorway, shirtless and carrying a briefcase and wearing combat boots, stepped onto the sidewalk to block us.

"I know who you are," he said to me, putting down his briefcase. He wore walking shorts and had thick legs. He was powerfully built. Isaac stepped back but was not alarmed.

"Who am I?" I asked.

"You're his bodyguard," he said.

"Who's he?" I asked.

"I don't know, but I saw him on the Merv Griffin show," he said. "And Dick Cavett."

"James Joyce," I said, and Isaac laughed—the first name in criminal obscurity to Isaac. The zealot in *The Penitent* speaks of Joyce and Eliot as what's wrong with literature.

"I've heard of James Joyce," the man said. "This isn't James Joyce." He stopped. "This is Isaac Singer," he said. "I'm a writer myself."

Singer said, "What do you write?"

The man said, "It's in my briefcase." He bent to open it, and I said, "Pal, we can't read it here on the sidewalk." I couldn't tell if he was a writer who would one day sweep all of us before him or a madman reaching for a bayonet or both.

He said, "What's the matter?"

I said, "Nothing, but it's time to move on."

He said, "I forgot. You're a bodyguard. Pretty tough, I guess."

"I've killed before," I said, "and I'll kill again."

The man stood back in astonishment, pulled his briefcase to him, and Isaac and I walked on. Isaac could not stop laughing. He caught his breath and laughed again.

"You told him you'd killed before!" he said. "That's what you told him? Please, say it again for me."

I said it again, and when Singer boarded his cab he said, "I've killed before and I'll kill again. Be well, my friend."

Another time we were walking near the Bal Harbour Shops up to the Singapore Hotel on Collins for a last cup of coffee. Singer was pale and had a bright pink flush to his upper cheeks. His eyes were watery. He had returned the night before from a speaking engagement and, like many other such occasions in the time I knew him, was exhausted from it. Our walk had tired him, but our conversation had revived him somewhat, and he said, "Come, we'll make the Singapore rich."

Preparing to cross the street on Harding, a thick man in Bermuda shorts below his knees and bursting out of a white polo shirt with an alligator at the breast, said, "Isaac Singer, Isaac Singer."

Isaac stopped and turned and said, "Yes, my friend."

"You don't know me, Mr. Singer," the man said. "My name is Ben Malofsky, and I heard you talk in Buffalo. I knew it was you."

We both waited. The man patted Isaac on the shoulder and said, "Well, keep up the good work."

Singer said, "Thank you, thank you." And he said to me, "See."

I had been lecturing him on wasting his energies on mad dashes across the country to speak, to read, to be a kind of comedian from the ashes. He was certainly loved, but at what price did he present himself to give people something to love?

"You know, Isaac," I said, "Dickens was a person like you and not just in his works. He couldn't stop performing. He'd do readings wherever he could find an audience. There's a certain scene in *Oliver Twist* where Bill Sykes kills Nancy, his mistress. It's a violent scene and it took a lot out of Dickens to do a stage reading of it, and his doctor told him he was in no condition to read the scene. But Dickens went ahead and read it and died shortly afterward. Now, Professor, what good will you do anybody if you're soon up in heaven with the other prophets from traveling to speak?"

"Stop, please, stop, don't lecture me. I hear enough from Alma."

Alma had described a recent trip of theirs to Cleveland. There was no one at the airport to meet them, and they stumbled around looking for a taxicab and then for a motel they barely knew the name of, and at the motel they found confusion about their reservation. And, finally on the stage, Isaac was awarded a medallion in a ceremony that lasted less than five minutes and not asked to speak. For no honorarium, it was a favor of some sort Isaac was repaying someone in his past.

When they occasionally asked me to travel with them, I said, bluntly, "No."

Arranging transportation with Isaac once for the two of us to go out to Santa Rosa, California, to visit our friend Bill Babula, Singer called me, by actual count, five times in two hours. First, I was not to book us on a DC anything; some had recently crashed and no DC anythings. Then he called to tell me he would not travel on any schedule that involved nighttime. Next, he said we'd stay no more than a day and a half rather than the three days and two nights we had agreed on. When he called for the eighth time, four days before we left, and said he was too ill to travel, I felt joy in every part of myself, and I called the unhappy Babula—who sent me the attractive posters he'd prepared for Singer's appearance—and I shouted, "Bill, we're not coming. You've been spared!"

At the Singapore a man and a woman came to stand over Singer as he had his coffee and I had my tea. They said they recognized him and had both read his work. The conversation trailed off after a while when the two people in the coffee shop ran out of things to say and Isaac had nodded at them until he tired. Then he looked away, and they said, "Thank you" and shook hands with both of us. Isaac made a gesture of presentation to me after the couple left.

There, he seemed to say with his hand, I'm wanted. The inconsequentiality of the encounter—it was obvious the two people had read little of his work—did not matter to him. Desperately lonely as he often told me he was, being famous was one of his few comforts.

I entered 1985 better able to bear Isaac and the chaos around him. Mrs. *Beautiful* was scheduled for publication in the summer. My middle son had married in a large, bountiful ceremony, and, while my sister had died in 1984 (on Isaac's birthday, July 14), I had come over the years to as harmonious a compromise with her as was possible in this life. My memories of her were not unkind; and what was there but memories now?

Loss, however, was everywhere. My friend at the university, John McCollum, who had hired me in 1960, took a long drive with me in December to where Deedee and I had discovered south of Miami a small, white coral church. John, a former Methodist minister, was assembling a book of photographs and historical commentary on the churches of Florida, and I wanted him to see the place. We came from lunch, an occasion for talk we had practiced for twenty-four years, sometimes once a week, sometimes three. We were running over the vagaries of human nature as we drove down U.S. Route 1 when a large rock came flying at the car from the side of the highway. The sound and feel of it striking John's side of the car was terrifying. By the indentation in the side of the car, had it hit a foot higher and through John's window, the consequences would have been tragic. We both remembered seeing a man on a tractor on the side of the road and the rock had obviously been thrown with such force from under the wheels of the tractor.

The church, it turned out, was familiar to John. It was two blocks away from the first church he had ministered when he came to Miami in about 1946. We walked around the building and he told me the age of the coral, the meaning in the windows, and the denomination that had probably first built it. He described the character of the people who worshiped there. We got back in the car after a while, and John said there was a post office on the left side of the country road we followed to get back on to the highway and he'd like to pick up some stamps for his Christmas mailings. It was the twentieth. I told him, "I like a man who attends to things on time."

At the post office I waited. John was gone for about ten minutes. I drove him home without incident, not talking about mortality or his escape from the huge thrown rock when we passed the place. I pulled into his driveway, and he said, "See you later." It was a lunch hour during my intersession workshop, and I pulled back out of his driveway without seeing him enter his house, and that was the last time I ever saw him. He died a few days later in a fall at his second home up at Lake Worth in central Florida.

He was my last link to the people and Miami as it had been when I was hired in 1960. He had hired me, and I wrote to Deedee, still in Pittsburgh, that I'd met a man with a remarkable control of syntax. Listening to McCollum was like taking a trip down the Amazon, with all its twists, shoals, and rapids: he started out sentences and, with an explorer's surefootedness and daring, made them come out in unexpected places at little hazard to diction. I had listened to him for decades. He had a reputation for sobriety, but I smile when I think of him, always something funny in my mind about his seriousness.

Singer, when he met him, whispered to me, "That man has a noble head."

I said, "He's my closest friend in Florida."

Isaac said, "You are very lucky to have such a man for a friend."

Of the thousands of memories of John, I remember him particularly at a grim party talking with great gravity to three admirers, his arms behind his back, rocking. I moistened a small napkin and walked up behind him and pressed it dripping wet into his hand and he did not miss a syllable or change his tone or cadence.

In the academic world we inhabited, with its own peculiar true north, he taught me the points of the compass we lived by: dignity and forbidden territory; what platitudes were incendiary, which safe; how we could thrive even in situations often calculated to destroy joy.

"If I couldn't write," Singer said to me one day after I told him about John's death, "I'd kill myself."

"That's what other artists say," I said. "Is it true?"

"Yes, I am in despair."

"About what?"

"Old age."

"But you were never cheerful even when you were young."

"I knew it would all come to nothing," he said.

Other artists might be self-contained or strange to behold, but Isaac Singer was so intact and inimitably himself that he had about him the quality of an artifact. It was an existentialist's authenticity.

Something else, too, was apparent after a while. He used his own separateness, the wit and despair and isolation, to make claims on other peoples' stereotypes of what they perceived him to be, what he *should* be for them. I was touched by him, too. This is not to say he didn't suffer; he did.

He so identified himself with Jews and being Jewish, admittedly his peculiarly candid and philosophically singular type, that news of Jews from anywhere touched him personally. I saw him cry only once: the day the confused word came that Israeli troops had gone into a Palestinian refugee camp and shot down people there. The restatement of the who and why of it had not been known then, and Singer thought there had been Jewish soldiers in the camp. He tried to talk to me about it, but broke down and sobbed, "We killed innocent men and women," he said. "Jews did it. It was us, not Nazis." I tried to console him, but I felt awful about it too so I just put my hand on his shoulder. "Jews, it was us," he said. "What has the world come to?"

Later that day, he started to say something funny, then checked himself. "I can't joke today, Lester," he said. "This is a terrible, black day for me," and he cut short our walk and went home. (In discussing himself as a writer, though, he said often, "I do not write as a Jew, and I do not write for Jewish audiences only." I find no contradiction between his identification of himself with Judaism—despite his quips about Jewish egomania and contentiousness—and his search for a universal voice in his fiction. I think he saw Yiddish itself for him as the closest he can come in language to the tongue of Everyman.)

I wanted him, as others did, to be the survivor of the Nazi's oppression, paradoxical that his gentleness and powerlessness would survive after a time of tanks and bombs and the victim triumphant. But he wasn't that either, not by the facts. He had, I believe, never seen a Nazi except in the newsreels or newspapers. He had, he told me, lost no one at all to Nazis. (I do not know where the account of his mother and sister dying at the hands of Nazis originated.) Yet audiences, and I suspect readers, identified him—quite accurately, if their observations were large enough—with dead Polish Jewry, all their stars dimmed by a bloodtide. But he himself as a personal survivor of death camps and privation was not the man he was, by many, understood to be.

He was in New York in 1935, but I too saw the loss when I looked at him. Who were the nameless others if this was not one of them? Often in his fear he played to others peoples' visions like a skillful matador, prodding them this way then that with his bright red cape, understanding them. They loved him for their reasons; he loved them for his. He understood the torments of our common anguish.

I said to Singer when we were discussing an article I'd written about him in the Miami Herald, about his unfounded Holocaust reputation—he said it was "the best article" anyone had ever written about him—"But there's another aspect to you, Isaac, that you can't deny." (I had come back to Miami from New York the week before after visiting the YIVO exhibit at the 92d Street "Y", "Image Before My Eyes," photographs of the Jews of Warsaw in the 1920s and 1930s.) "You're a reminder of what was destroyed by the Germans even if you yourself did not die or live the terrible experiences that some survivors did. Seeing you, reading your work, is a reminder that the Jews of Poland and everywhere else in Europe were more than victims of mass murder. They were vital, interesting people in their lives. They had triumphs, concerns, adventures before them, sorrows and joy behind them. To me it is as if you and your brother were those men in the photographs."

"Will I be remembered that way?" he asked.

"By me anyhow. That's who you are, a Jew from Warsaw who was one of those people in the pictures. Maybe some others escaped—you did, thank God. They live in you."

"You're very kind, my friend," he said. "It's true."

Square-jawed gymnasts in white with their smooth muscles, the dark-eyed actresses and producers with coats over their shoulders like capes, horn-rimmed writers and intellectuals sitting alone or in groups staring into the camera, owl-like, as if they studied the camera and the future rather than the camera them.

～ Chapter Six

THE CONFERENCE ROOM where we held class, with Isaac bewildered about *The Penitent* and not too clear in his own mind about his objectives in forsaking fiction and autobiography for argument, magnified his university problems. His warmth and curiosity about people overwhelmed him. A class would patiently wait and then break off as he found a reason to turn to someone on his left or right or to a visitor and hold a lengthy discussion with them. We all overheard an intense conversation a woman held with him about a trip to Israel. Another time he spoke to a student about Eastern Europe. Somewhere in his innate love of character—for him it was narrative—he contrived to practice his other skill, earning love. The distances of classroom decorum vanished: Isaac Singer played love songs under the windows of uncomprehending undergraduates.

"We are not here to be hits," I said after class.

He nodded as if he had the situation under control. "We're not supposed to be loved," I told him as, infatuated by the proximity of students, he shamelessly pitched them in elfin smiles, sly withdrawals, lavish praise, and interest enough in a hapless coed to justify her thinking her horoscope had been correct that morning. In the conference room, starting with a genuine affection for oddity and the common tragedy that stalked the human race, with pity and terror he sang his feelings of loneliness, courting our class. Sometimes too enchanted by the voices and presences, he had to stir himself as if from sleep to say something about their fiction—in short, act like a teacher instead of a mooning swain. He flattered young men as well as women with his attention, but for women he almost fell from his chair, leaning forward, his Adam's apple bobbing, his face flushed, and his eyes glittering as an old want for connection was subtly satisfied.

He became so involved in the classroom procedures—when he was not lost to us in the almost unimaginable thoughts that carried him away from any present human contact—that he responded to the stories in class with an unbounded enthusiasm. The enthusiasm covered his adverse opinions, as well as his friendly appraisals. He would blurt out, as the student finished reading, "This is a masterpiece. I wish I could write like this when I was young." Or he would say: "These are, my friends, boring, trivial people and this is a boring, trivial story. I wish I could say better but it is not a story."

After I explained to him the difficulties I had with his outbursts, he said he would remember not to do it. "The point is if I talk first that'll give you a chance to collect your thoughts," I said, "maybe to get a better handle on the story by what I say. It won't leave me in the position of disagreeing with you all the time. You're the honored guest, you should have the last word. I won't talk long, I promise. I'll say what I have to say in such a way it'll be like an introduction for you."

He agreed. He said, "Yes, my friend!" a dozen times when I brought it up. But now frequently he said in his outbursts, "Dr. Goran doesn't want me to talk first, but I must, this story is a little masterpiece. I say it and I mean it."

Often, when I spoke—after his panegyric—he simply said, "Anybody else?" and pointed in the direction of the class. We had agreed—a hundred times—that I would call on students, since he couldn't see them.

When he called out, "Anybody else!" I said, "I'll be through in an hour, Professor, be patient," and sometimes he might laugh, but other times he ignored me. "Next, please!" he'd say over my voice, as if a milling crowd demanded to be heard, while students either snickered, were shocked, or stayed lethargic.

A student in the conference room submitted a story that semester about a *shtetl* and Jews who ran into the woods while angry gentile hoodlums pursued them. Singer sat silently while I talked about the story, pretending it was not a blatant imitation of Singer's time and place. The student who wrote it wanted to be a rabbi. Singer broke his silence to say, "The story is about nothing. The story is nothing." In my fumbling I said the story lacked authenticity of detail. Later, the student told me he so loved Singer's work that he thought he'd be pleased to be imitated, the sort of mistake inexperienced young people make. I explained to him that Singer probably thought he was being mocked.

But Isaac explained to me that Sunday, "An American can not imagine the brutality of peasants, of ruffians. I know. I saw such scenes I can't even write them and this was before Nazis."

"Aren't all sensitive people impressed with terrible scenes when they're young?" I asked.

"What can Americans know?"

"Isaac, I saw things I can't write about."

"So," he said, "they were American things."

"Do you really believe brutality has a different quality across national borders?"

"No, but only a Polish peasant acts like one."

Shortly after, I brought up the subject again, and I said, "Isaac, I don't think you understand life in an American slum. It's not as if American hoodlums dance in the streets in real life. Life was terrifying for us."

"I know, I know," he said. We sat on a bench in the Bal Harbour Shops mall.

"We were hunted like rats," I said. "We never fought back. We ran. We were afraid of our shadows."

"Stop. Stop!" he said, putting his hands to his ears. "Don't you know I can't bear to face such things."

I had forgotten: he was an attenuated, vibrating reed who trembled with every breeze of the world's pain, and I really was a callous nuisance (at the least) to provoke him. In our daily exchanges in class it was easy not to remember who he was at heart.

I told him a long story about a man in my neighborhood in Pittsburgh who got a twelve-year-old girl pregnant and then performed an abortion on her. Isaac relaxed as we left the ferocity of my early years in the fifth ward of Pittsburgh. The child, my friend, had died, and her family walked around in a daze for years vowing vengeance and seeking comfort—and found neither. The killer thrived, whispered about but respectable and healthy. There was no retribution for him or any unhappiness.

Singer said quietly, "If God punished us for our sins He'd have nothing else to do."

The next year, 1985, I had assembled us in a classroom with tiered seats that gave the room the quality of an amphitheater, and in our first week Alma attended class. Our first two weeks were always devoted to a jolly round of questions by the class and me with Isaac responding with quips and jests.

The spell of those first weeks often lingered with many students for the rest of the semester, the sense and presence of him. I asked a young woman, usually very critical of the university, the world, and herself, why she'd never complained about his treatment of her. She had written a story about a woman who tries on tight-fitting clothes before a mirror trying to decide whether she's going to seduce a mechanic who is fixing her car. Singer, who was an ocean and sixty years away in his inattention, asked, startled when she finished reading, "This girl, why doesn't she buy clothes that fit?"—his only response.

"It was Isaac Singer," she said, "talking about me. I know he wasn't listening. He could have said 'Good morning,' and I'd have been thrilled."

In the first week Alma answered questions too. On our way back to the limousine, a promenade from class to the fountain made up of long stops and slow surveys of buildings and grounds, she said, "They are really nice people, these students. I don't see why you have such trouble with them, Lester."

"I don't . . . " I started, and changed my mind. "I'm glad it was such a good experience. Come again soon, whenever you can find time."

Students had gathered about her after class, and she did come again the third week, but this time we had stories to criticize. Isaac sat at the desk while a student sat with him, or—a bad idea—stood over him at a podium reading. I sat along the wall in profile to the class, facing him and the student. Alma wanted to sit in a chair in front of the class and turn it to face the class. I walked across the room and leaned on a window sill as the class filed in. Then I said to myself, "Screw it," and went to Alma and asked her if she'd mind sitting in a chair among the class. It had occurred to me that if Isaac said something peculiar with her sitting in front of the class her grimace or cluck would attract attention, and the whole class, if not the world, would join us in our Sunday breakfast follies.

She asked, "Why?"

I said, "It's a classroom situation."

"I sat here before," she said.

"Today we're taking up student stories."

"So?"

"So I have to comment."

"So comment. I'm not bothering you."

"Leave this to me," I said. "You'll be more comfortable there."

"There were two chairs here last time," she said. "What did you do with the other chair?"

"I gave it to the Goodwill."

She stood and said, "I'll sit wherever you tell me. I'm a guest here. But you don't make sense, Lester."

"Thank you, Alma," I said and led her to a student who stood instantly, like a guard at Buckingham Palace, and shook hands, delighting her beyond measure with his interest. But she never came to the class again. I had crossed some line with her.

The most unhappy encounter that semester, though, occurred with a lightning-struck young woman Isaac had heaped praise on for a very negligible story. He began with his affection for stories about waitresses, waiters, hostesses in restaurants, and cashiers. He did not know much about how Americans earned their daily bread. He did not seem to think much about people not in the kind of places or times he knew about. He could translate waitresses or butchers or bakers or bankers.

I was stinting in my regard for the young woman's story. It had been written, I thought, with little interest in the nuances of thought or speech of any restaurant hostess on earth. The hostess thought things like, "Gee whiz!" or other anachronisms, synthetic, seemingly hard-boiled but sentimental, television tough-guy talk of the fifties. Singer, who had once wanted to use the phrase "Scram out of here" in one of his stories we worked on, was susceptible to her story. The combination of seemingly authentic slang and interest in a hostess by the student caused him to call this "a little masterpiece." The class knew it wasn't; so did I. The student, casting about for a lifesaver on stormy seas, clung to Singer's words; I would have done the same had I written such a story. But Isaac was too easily delighted sometimes. He exulted over words like "clobber," which I explained to him one day. He liked the expression "out of sight." He liked "buzz off" and "get out of town." Without resistance, he fell over himself in the student's sweep of fifty years of outdated language and my-feet-are-killing-me kind of hostess prose.

The student came bright and fresh to my office a month later to work out with me the details of her forthcoming triumphant collection of short stories, a quick walk to her M.A. There were in her arsenal two other stories, both with various problems, one promising, the other incoherent. She asked, "When can I begin?"

I said, "Any time. But you'll have to do better than the things I've seen."

She was, quite correctly, first incredulous—Isaac Singer, fool! This is Isaac Singer you challenge! Secondly, she was angry. What did I mean? How could I refuse a little masterpiece? Did I think I knew everything?

At that time, before we tightened our rules, I could, and did, say, "It's not necessary to work with me on this. Find someone else in the department, set up a committee, and impress them."

"What will you have to do with it?" she asked.

"Absolutely nothing."

It was a condition I aspired to in most of my dealings with Isaac as mentor to the young. As to the young woman, she could not find— did not try perhaps, on sober reflection—a committee to endorse her fiction. She had, worse lot, lost the trust she had been raised on since childhood: believe in your name brand. If the Nobel Prize on the novel did not constitute a warranty on the product, could General Motors be next? But the label was truthful. It was stamped on his own writing, not on his ability—or honest interest—in judging hers.

I understood her dilemma. On some days after translating with him, bored by the routine yet exhilarated, I had observed Singer, between dippiness and genius, create art.

Within minutes of my departure from the dismal game room some Sundays, I walked out on the beach behind his condominium building. The sun shone on the waves and I looked out over the ocean. The mysteries of art were endless, and, squinting my eyes to observe the ocean, there wasn't an answer there. I had read and accepted the man who created the art inside the Surfside Towers for twenty-five years. Who was the stranger who lurched and tap-danced, often so gracelessly, through our university lives?

The remorseless praise came often as the apology bouquet to the class after a particular cruel outburst. I thought at one time he was annoyed by tall blonde women; but I was wrong. In the semester of his erratic swings, angel wings the previous year now not even a memory, he attacked both a blonde woman and one with long dark hair. What had they in common? Could it be that they both stood at a podium reading? Both were relatively tall. Was he offended that they overshadowed him as he sat munching on a hard roll? I will never know.

The dark-haired woman, originally from Colombia, was a serious writer, interested in Marquez and her own fantastic visions of good and evil. Her story was characterized by eloquent language and absorbing images. Singer simply announced that the story did not have a beginning, a middle, and an end. I pointed out to the class

Lena's gifts for language, the meaning of the story, and then Ms. Toro sat down. I knew her well enough to apologize to her at the break. She was philosophical. "I knew he wouldn't like it," she said. "It's not your fault."

With the next woman's story that day, he declaimed against "such women" as this, blurring the characters in the story with the author. The story was a reminiscence, with time sequences reassembled to make its point about the author's theme. The author was direct about the sexuality of the college women in the story, and Isaac was inflamed. The only thing worse than his inattention was when he listened and caught certain details and held on to them like a cat with a ball of crackling cellophane. He said that the women in the story were not typical of women generally and no one could read such a story and identify with the characters, and it wasn't a story at all. No recognition here at all of his obtuseness that had mysteriously been apparent to him in the Oudens story. He was ready to publish *The Penitent* again.

I followed the student out of the classroom during the break. She was walking with her head down, angry and confused. "Marian," I said, "you know he can be off the wall sometimes."

"Someone ought to do something about him," she said.

I said, "It's a good story. You know it is. I know it is. Most of the class knows it is."

She was a public-school teacher who had returned to the university for additional credits and was articulate about literary subjects and, I believe, loved literature and once even Isaac Singer.

"How can he do this?" she asked, and I had no answer.

She did not drop the course, and when I chided him after class about mixing up authors and their characters he said he did no such thing. When I reminded him of the story we'd just heard, he did not remember what he'd said for a long time. When he did, he again lectured me as we walked to the limo about women.

"They are such whores," he said. He shook with rage, his face dark. "They are such scum. They are unbearable, my friend. They are low.

They take all, they give nothing. They are a scandal to God. What they have made of the world is a garbage dump."

I said, "I agree with you."

"You do?" he asked. The walk down the path to the fountain where the limousine waited was dappled in sunlight.

"They're just like men," I said, and he approved of the irony. He laughed. "That's right, that's right, we're all pigs."

In *The Penitent* he offers at the end in his own name a careful half-renunciation of the violence to logic and the assault on common sense that has preceded it in the book. He says that while many will not agree with the solution Shapiro finds in the book—the cracked community of saints, Judaism beyond Judaism, promised land inside Israel itself—there's no denying that Shapiro has accurately appraised the modern world. He loathed advertising and publishers, airplanes and college professors (who reviewed his books), leftists, Manachem Begin and Elie Wiesel, Alma a fair share of the time, and liberals— preceded always by "phony."

What he liked, he told me, were policemen. He said, "Policemen are the only people in society who still believe in it. They risk their lives to protect it."

"Some are crooked," I said.

"Yes, but less of them are crooked than in other professions. Doctors, lawyers, teachers are all crooks, swindlers."

"I agree with you about policemen as a group. I think all the professions have individuals who try to do good, but I think policemen are almost all there is for society in general. Except one. I think nurses are like policemen, they hold society together."

He did not respond.

"Come on Isaac, why leave out nurses?" I asked.

"Your experience is different than mine."

"You had a bad experience with nurses?"

"Only policemen believe in society," he said.

Another time I told him I had been in the military police. I described our life there, the breaking up of fights, the chases in our Jeeps after fugitives in the Virginia woods, the stockades with the marching prisoners, the informers, the cold winds on traffic details. He listened, hanging on every word, then said, "Imagine a Jew in the military police! Imagine. A Jew in the army. There were other Jews there in the army?"

"In the army quite a few," I said. "Not so many in the military police."

"Ah, the Jews don't want to be policemen?"

"I don't know. I knew a few."

"You were all friends?"

"No," I said, "they weren't friends."

He struck off one of his life epiphanies better left to literature. "Jews are always happier being enemies with each other than friends."

"I just didn't like these guys," I said. "They didn't like me."

"You liked gentiles better."

"No, I didn't have many friends at all in the military police," I said. "It wasn't a place for friendships. They all turned each other in to the officers. It was a miserable experience. The stockades had barbed wire. I used to listen to the prisoners marching all night; our barracks was just outside the prison."

"And the other Jewish policemen? They turned you in?"

"No, they weren't the spies. We all knew the spies, we avoided them. I don't remember that any of the Jews were spies, just jerks."

"Jerks?"

"Yes, there was a kid named Plotkin. The other soldiers said he wet his bed. They said he cried in his sleep."

"Jews are not soldiers."

"There were gentiles they said wet their beds too."

"But you were not friends with Plotkin."

"No, he tried too hard to make friends with everybody. He was tiring."

"There were other Jews."

"One other, I remember: a Margolies."

"He complained too?"

"No, he was a big tough kid from Brooklyn. He was friendly and everybody liked him—as much as those guys could—but we weren't friends."

"Two Jews, you couldn't be friends?"

"He was a moron."

"So the Jews were morons and complainers."

"Neither of the Jews was perfect. I was."

"You had no friends in the police?"

"One guy I particularly liked. He was shipped up to Alaska. He wrote me, but I was too guilty to answer. I got out of going to Alaska by playing basketball. They took me off orders to go to Alaska and the guy—his name was Trembley—cried because we were going to be separated, and I was so happy I was almost laughing but I couldn't show it. I didn't want to go to Alaska. I missed Trembley, but I didn't want to go to Alaska. So when he wrote me I was too guilty to answer."

Singer sat listening intently, and I asked, "Aren't you going to say Jews in the army get out of going to Alaska by playing basketball?"

He barely laughed. "Jews in the military police," he said. "Imagine. Who could dream such things in Poland?"

One night in April before I came down to see him on a Sunday, I had a nightmare about a scene in my novel *Mrs. Beautiful*. In it black men are set afire by guards at the pressed-steel car plant where they are being held captive by the company as strikebreakers. When they rush to the gates of the plant they are doused with gasoline, set on fire, and sent running through the streets of McKees Rocks ablaze. It really did happen in 1908, and it kept me awake until morning when I shaved and went down to meet Isaac.

As we walked up Collins a man came toward us from the other direction. He was wearing a yachting cap, a tie, and buttoned-up suit and he swung an umbrella. Casually, I said to Isaac, "Here's the captain now."

The man stopped us. He stood in our paths and poked the umbrella toward me and said, "You're bringing these niggers to Surfside. They're going to be running through the streets here just like they do up north. Well, we're not going to have it. We've got guns too and we've got knives."

He didn't touch us with the umbrella but he was coming close. He jabbed in the direction of Singer who fell behind me. I asked, "What's the matter with you?"

"I know what's on your mind!" he said.

"Forget about it," I said, and pushed Isaac along, the two of us walking quickly. I waited for the man to shout more at me, but, when we came to the curb to cross to the Bal Harbour Shops and I turned to look back down Collins, he was gone.

Singer was angry with me.

"You must guard what you're thinking!" he said.

"That man can't know what I'm thinking."

"You think it plenty," he said. "Everybody knows what you're thinking."

It was the Isaac Singer of imps behind mirrors, and he was telling me I mustn't incite street madmen with thoughts from my novel. I had never had such an experience before. Without him, I expect it'll never happen again.

When a review of *Mrs. Beautiful* appeared in *The New Yorker* in October, Isaac was in Surfside, but he didn't call me and I didn't call him. The review described the book as "a strong and shapely novel by a translator of Isaac Bashevis Singer" and took note of the numerous errors on the dust jacket, calling the edition "slapdash." The review closed with: "Mr. Goran's focus is on the strike, and his portrayal of tragic passions—passions that can work only minor miracles—rivals Mr. Singer's darker plots."

I knew Isaac wouldn't like it.

I'd been compared in reviews of my other books, before I knew Singer, to Kafka, Bellow, Wolfe, Sterne, and Fielding (I have them right here!) and Singer too. When I finally saw him—the longest period between visits we had in his Florida years—he did not mention the review, and I finally asked him if he saw it (since I often read him his reviews), and he said that he had. "They do us both a compliment," he said, and the novel was never again mentioned by either of us to the other.

While the Singer class was still a week away, Barry Farber asked me on his radio program in New York, "Now Isaac Singer and you are two civilized men, you're sophisticated. How on earth do two people like the two of you dare to represent yourselves as teaching the art of writing fiction to anyone?"

Farber's program was one of the places I visited in January 1986 on a talk-show tour arranged for me by New Horizons, the publishers of *Mrs. Beautiful*. Joan Dunphy, the publisher, and her husband, Dermit, lived out on Long Island, and I stayed at their apartment on the Upper East Side for a few days.

When I went to respond to Farber's provocative question, I couldn't talk. My tongue attached to the roof of my mouth and stayed glued there. I moistened my mouth until I could speak, and Farber looked at me with concern. I don't remember what I said, but it was an interesting night. Roy Innis of CORE (Congress of Racial Equality) and a friend of his were there, as well as a stock analyst who, it turned out, had once been convicted of a sex crime. Talking to Bob Swaim the next day on CBS Radio, I had to ask for water; I still couldn't get my tongue loose from the roof of my mouth. In my last talk-show appearance, with the late Pegeen Fitzgerald of Public Radio, she kept handy a small pitcher of water. She also had a gift for me. A famous conservative, she gave me a souvenir that had been in her family, an IWW songbook. She had liked *Mrs. Beautiful* and the radicals in it—she saw them for the independent spirits they were—and rewarded me with the book and some excellent company for the hour and a half I spent with her answering calls. *Mrs. Beautiful* had come out of the gate fast.

Back in Miami I urinated six times a night and decided the old advice my sergeant, Bill Eaton, had given me was true. Attending a wedding with me—the bride and groom, professional singers, sang light opera in the ceremony and a chorus supported them—Sergeant Eaton said wistfully, "You know, corporal, it's all a race with your prostate, no matter how we dress up life." Now, I thought, I've lost the race. The derailing of the prostate, like the arrival of the barbarians at the gate of Athens, signaled the end.

I gave my diagnosis to Dr. Ray Mummery, my physician, who asked, "What's your other guess?"

"I want it to be nerves first. Then I guess diabetes if it isn't going to be nerves. Last, I want it to be the prostate."

It wasn't nerves and it wasn't the prostate; it was a diabetes that would require no medication either by injection or orally. It could be controlled by eating certain foods in appropriate amounts. The dryness, the blurring of the eyes, which I took for old age, and the frequent visits to the men's room vanished when I changed my eating habits, but I discovered another hazard.

A dizziness occurs in people with my condition when they move too quickly, usually after a meal. My first attack came when Deedee and I, finishing breakfast in a restaurant, ran across a street in South Miami to escape a sudden rain shower. The ground grew larger and came up after me. The dizziness can occur with stress: glucose up, then quickly down, and welcome to the sawdust. Together with my beta-blocker, Inderal, a famous source of vertigo, and now diabetes, I had a double possibility for sinking into darkness. The low blood sugar is called hypoglycemia; the high is hyperglycemia. The drop from one to another is called a fainting spell, something I'd never experienced—but always possible when one hears a great writer say for the thousandth time to a class, "I learned a lot today, students, believe me."

Not two weeks into the new semester, our grace period, I received a call at my office from a man speaking English but with a Yiddish accent so thick I could hardly understand him. He shouted into the phone and told me he was a visiting scholar from Boston. Would it be possible to arrange a meeting with Isaac Singer? I told him that Mr. Singer was at the university on Mondays and perhaps he could talk to him at the break—which I'd extend to fifteen minutes—or meet with him for a few minutes after class. "*Before he takes his limousine!*" I shouted back.

"*I said a meeting! A meeting! A meeting!*"

"*What do you mean a meeting?*"

Going into the field with cartons of juice, cookies, and an occasional egg-salad sandwich, all sent by Alma, Singer's Monday classes were often carnivals of spilled food, talking, and chewing.

"*Who is this?*"

"President Reagan," I said in a normal tone, and when he didn't answer I knew the shouting came from his own hearing disabilities. "*Mr. Singer's valet!*" I shouted.

"*I want a meeting!*"

"*See you Monday, one-thirty.*"

"*Not this Monday!*" He began to reel off his schedule in Miami until May, when he was returning to Boston. Whatever he concluded as to when he was coming, I shouted "*My pleasure!*" hung up, and quickly forgot the call. Under the lava at Pompeii are people waiting for men such as this bristling scholar to work them into their plans.

In a particularly noisy class three weeks later, I called the students to order while Singer sat behind me sipping cranapple juice from a carton with what looked like a half-eaten hard roll and a mangled caterpillar lying in a napkin on the desk. He would move the food aside when a student came to the front to read his or her story. "Okay," I said, "okay, let's get started."

Someone asked, "Will we get any written remarks on our stories?" and I said, "I'll be happy to say something if you'd like."

A small man in a vest came in the door near the back of the class. The shirt under the vest lay in small bubbles, and the suit jacket was several sizes too small. Warty, wearing thick glasses and a hearing aid, he walked past me without a word, as I stood before the desk where Singer sat behind me. Beamer circled the desk behind me and said, *"Dr. Beamer from Boston!"*

"Who? What?" Singer asked, looking up from his juice carton.

"Beamer! Beamer!" the man said. *"I'm a friend of Gershon's!"* [not the name he used].

"Ah, Gershon, Gershon."

I said to the class, my voice rising, "One of the things we haven't talked about much this semester is 'voice.' " I was seizing the moment, a rare opportunity for banned creative writing talk during a Singer semester. " 'Voice' is a very important component of fiction; sometimes in contemporary fiction it's virtually all there is."

"Gershon is dead!" the visiting scholar said behind me.

"What? What?" Singer asked.

"Your friend in Boston."

"Yes, well, everyone dies," Singer said.

"He was a man respected by all who knew him," the scholar announced in Yiddish. "Cards and flowers came from all over the world. He left only grandchildren and great-grandchildren. His wife has been dead forty years."

Singer answered in Yiddish, "I didn't know him well."

"I'm hard of hearing!" Dr. Beamer proclaimed in English.

"What?"

I tried to talk, louder each time. I looked back at the two men. "Gentlemen, we're ready to begin class."

Singer asked the man, "You're a Yiddish scholar?"

Phyllis Shaw, a high-school teacher who sat in the front row, leaned forward and said to me, "This will teach you to be serious."

Behind me I heard the buzz of Yiddish, small laughs of appreciation. Then Dr. Beamer asked, "So, *nu?* What do you think of the future of Yiddish altogether?"

I said to the class, "Let's take a ten-minute break now, no break later."

When Dr. Beamer left a few minutes later he did not speak to me but strode out the class and down the corridor as purposefully as he had entered. He walked tilted backward, satisfied. The conversation had gone well. He had spoken to Isaac Singer down in Miami and, if the future of Yiddish was imperiled, at least it was not, like the late Gershon, dead.

Singer did not ask—as I expected—after the scholar left, "Why do you let such people in here?" He said instead, as the students returned to their seats, "He's a famous Yiddish scholar, that man," nodding his head.

"Tell me," he asked later, "what was that lunatic's name?"

The following Sunday, while Isaac was detained, Alma and I had a discussion about the nature of nobility. She had come down to tell me he would be late. Usually he and I ate alone. He became angry when I brought someone with me or saw someone that I knew in Danny's (mostly students) and they came over to talk to me. Once I brought my son Bobby who had been consumed by the prospect of meeting him. I had told Singer he was coming and he seemed agreeable, but he said nothing to Bobby all through breakfast. It took me three weeks to get Singer to agree to meet James Michener, who was visiting the university, for breakfast. He directly said, "He's come to take my job," and laughed.

"He won't be here that long," I said. "He's a world traveler. He stops at a university for a couple of years, then moves on."

"You brought him here?" he asked.

"No," I said, "the president did. I don't bring anyone here, Isaac. I'm just a faculty member."

"No one asked you about it?"

"I didn't bring him, but I thought it would be a good thing when I was told about it."

"You don't want me? The President doesn't want me?"

"Wrong."

That Sunday, as Alma and I waited for Isaac, she claimed that the only friend she had in Surfside Towers was the doorman: she and he were both Germans and were not jealous of each other. They understood each other. I said that I thought these differences were exaggerated when it came to discussing relations between nationalities of Jews in America in modern times.

"You don't think some people are more refined than other people?" she asked.

"Mostly environmental," I said.

"Ach! And Isaac says you're intelligent."

"He's right."

"Then why don't you know some people are born with refinements?"

"Some things people are born with, some not."

"What about Grace Kelly?"

"She's an example of what?"

"Don't you think she was born a princess? Every inch of her, she was so beautiful and so refined, beautiful clothes and jewelry."

"She married the prince of a bogus country," I said. "How does that make her born a princess—or even a princess now?" I warmed up. "Do you know that in Monaco the royalty there gets a rake-off from prostitution, gambling. Your princess is nothing better than a madam, living off the earnings of prostitutes."

"Princess Grace is a prostitute?"

"I don't know. Is she?"

"She's a princess! Don't you know anything?"

"I think she's beautiful," I said.

"She has an inner beauty."

"And she was born with that?"

"Yes. She was born a princess," Alma said.

"I liked her in *High Noon*."

"What's *High Noon*?"

"A western. A great cowboy movie."

"She was never in such a movie," Alma said, more outraged by cowboys than my charge of royal pandering, as Isaac joined us. "Isaac," she said, "Lester says Princess Grace was a cowboy actress."

Isaac, in a jovial mood, said, "So she's the first cowboy-cowgirl."

Alma, still simmering, said, "He says she's a madam."

"Who?" he asked.

"Grace Kelly."

"I never heard of her," he said.

"A harlot," I said.

Alma said, "You're crazy, do you know that? You should watch what you say."

"Get a license for being crazy," Isaac said, reaching for my orange juice. "Then it's legal."

I had been on sabbatical in the fall of 1985. It brought the advent of a new chairman of English, Zack Bowen. A new dean brought in Bowen, and our department acquired three other new people in either tenure-track or senior positions.

At first amused, Singer asked, "Who are all those people? Where will they find offices for them?"

He was less pleased when I told him they were mostly Joyce specialists. We were to be a sort of Joyce center, publishing a Joyce periodical.

"You wanted this?" he asked.

He still harbored the suspicion that I ran the University of Miami—my letting him escape two or three weeks early every year without penalty—and that I was probably a crypto-Joycean spy among the Chekovians. My loyalty to the nineteenth century, even with a Henry James thesis at Pitt, seemed very shaky to him. I had told him often that I thought Joyce was a great writer: he mustn't blame Joyce for the people who had made an extraliterary game of him. There was power in Joyce, even of the traditional sort Tolstoy could recognize.

"No, my side lost," I said. "I was on Russo's side. The Joyce thing was an afterthought. New chairmen from outside usually change the direction of a department."

He almost rocked in place with sorrow. "My days are numbered."

"That's not true," I said.

"Any place with so many Joyces doesn't want me."

"Joyce has always been here. I teach Joyce in my contemporary literature class."

He sat back, too stunned to speak. "You teach students Joyce? You talk about him?"

"Isaac, Kafka too. Eliot, Auden, Stevens."

He recovered and shook his head. "They are *experimentalists*, phonies. With Kafka one is enough. Why do you teach young people to write like him?"

"I'm not teaching anybody to write like anybody," I said. "This is a literature class. I teach Isaac Singer in the class too."

"Take me out. Those fakers will bury me."

On literary subjects I had a surprise call from him one day while he was in New York. His calls usually had at their core the not-very-subtle question "Are you hiding a check of mine down there?" and he was never quite satisfied by my answer. Tonight, excited, he said, "Listen, Lester, I was just talking to a lady professor and she is an expert. She told me Henry James is very difficult to understand. She said he is an elitist."

"Isaac, it's a matter of opinion. If he were too difficult, how could I understand him?"

"No, no, I didn't know you're an elitist."

"I'm not a Republican," I said, an old joke of ours. I found a card sent to him from the Republican party in mail he'd asked me to look over. An accompanying letter thanked him for his contribution. In mock seriousness, but meaning it, he said, "When you write a biography of me, please don't put this in."

The lady professor had puzzled him. I had explained to him that many of Henry James's themes were similar to his own. He had listened fascinated to the narratives of "The Jolly Corner" and "The Beast in the Jungle." He had decided after I recounted the plot of "The Aspern Papers" and "The Turn of the Screw" that he and James were, if not kindred spirits, at least two men who could get along. He was, it seems though, much more interested in the relationship between Henry and his elder brother, William. Henry was always respectful. William misunderstood Henry's life and work. I did not introduce him to this subject; he asked me about the brothers when I first told him about my interest in Henry James.

I informed Bowen that I wasn't happy about working with Isaac, and he told me he understood. "I'm leaving this all up to you," he said. And there it stood: Singer feeling like a lost settler on the frontier with Joyce scholars, like so many Apaches, racing around his ever-shrinking campfire.

Isaac had never been a great source of interest among the university faculty. I repeatedly invited the faculty—ours, anybody's—to sit in on our class sessions, but few came. At his university-wide appearances many more people from the community attended than did students or faculty. His salary came from a special fund, not from our departmental budget. If it had, I'm sure there would have been carnage with reminders, bitter and profound, that we were under-staffed in the renaissance and medieval periods, had no one in linguistics, did not teach at all at that time Greek and Roman classics in translation.

At Singer's small parties, held for him in the conference room by the department when he came back each spring, he sat by himself. An occasional grad student joined him to exchange jokes. The parties were crowded. I brought all the undergraduates I could find. Except for a few members of the department who read and admired him—a sort of guilty nonacademic pleasure—he was no great event among us.

On my identification with Isaac over the years, a colleague said to me, "People at the university have hardly ever thought of you as Jewish. Why do you want to adopt Jewishness now?"

Not having the resources to explain that, for all of Singer's subject matters so ingrained with old Jewish life and his ultimately Jewish sensibility, his enormous resources of literary virtuosity and energy made him now like Hardy or Gogol to me, Twain or Dickens rather than Sholem Aleichem, with whom he also had literary kinship.

Singer and I spoke once of a man who had written a sort of mythical history of the Jews and at the last recited an account of his family.

I said, "He wrote a history of Jews and ended it with himself."

"If he could," Isaac said, "he'd like to have begun the history with himself."

As Isaac paid the bill one Sunday at Danny's, Alma took my arm and said, "I can't go on."

Things at school had seemed fairly normal for Isaac and me, and I was puzzled.

Alma's alarm was in her customary apocalyptic tone. She said, "He is driving me crazy." (He, of course, said this of her.) "It's impossible."

"Alma, it's an old story."

"He gets into the bathtub with his clothes on."

I said, "He's just forgetful. Is this new?"

"No, he's always been forgetful—I can't stand it anymore."

"Just watch him," I said.

"I watch him night and day. Listen, before he goes to school with you, he puts on all his clothes and then he puts on his pajamas and wants to leave the house. Here he comes!"

If he had become more erratic in recent months I could not testify to it. He seemed himself to me. Our sessions at "translating" were, if anything, going better than usual. He was sharp and attentive, inventive, and he filled in the time between our work sessions in the game room with anecdotes and questions and good cheer. He tired more easily, but perhaps it was me. The diabetes let me know when I was pushing a morning too far.

I told Alma about my diabetes and said, "I'd like to meet Isaac at nine instead of nine thirty. I don't eat from five the day before. I can get woozy."

"It must be nine thirty!" she said. "He can't make it before nine thirty."

"Well, I'll have breakfast at eight, my usual time," I said, "then I'll join him for coffee afterward."

"Listen, I see you eat the same things you always eat," she said, testing me, resentment there, and suspicion. "You also don't eat salads. You should eat salads."

"I have a salad with dinner, and why shouldn't I eat what I always eat? As long as there's no sugar in the food. I never did eat much sugar. Salads have nothing to do with diabetes."

She laughed with appreciation of my stupidity. "You got diabetes and you didn't eat sugar much? Lester, diabetes comes from eating sugar. You eat chocolate cake."

"Alma, you've never in your life seen me eat chocolate cake."

"Do you swim?"

"Not for a few years."

"Ah, you should swim."

"Okay, I'll swim."

"Lester, you are making yourself a sick man. There's nothing wrong with you. You're a young man."

"You're right," I said. "Nine o'clock."

"Impossible, it cannot be done."

When she continued to insist that I come at nine thirty or ten o'clock for the rest of the time I knew her, I said after a while, "I can't, I'll fall into a coma," or "I'll undergo a personality change if I do."

But I was her friend and closest ally up to a point. She mistrusted Isaac's secretary in New York more than she did me. In a contest between the two of us—the secretary did "translating" too—I won.

Alma approved of Isaac working with me; she felt his secretary influenced him too heavily—obviously I was not a man to persuade anyone into anything. She knew he didn't pay me, and that was a dream she shared with Isaac.

When I first came routinely on Sundays she bustled around their apartment, demanding we work there. She made me tea and cleared away papers from either the dining-room table or his desk near a balcony. Her early feeling that I had usurped her place as his translator evaporated. After his nephew Joseph Singer had resigned, she decided I was not an adventurer, not even someone, bless the boy, who wanted any money at all for his chores. If I was not the ghost of Rachel MacKenzie to her, I was at least a chauffeur and old shoe. But the stuffy game room downstairs as a working place was preferable to both Isaac and me. It was not her continuing presence (she vanished on errands of her own the minute we were settled), there was something too convivial about the bright apartment. The sun shone on the ocean outside and the pale walls reflected light. The dark decor of Isaac's fiction could find few American settings where its creation would seem in order. His apartment in New York was appropriately dark: old furniture, green velour, refinished wood. Downstairs in the condo with a senile blonde woman who wandered in and spoke to us, cries of neighborly owners recounting travels to early-bird specials in Dania, a maintenance man who checked us frequently, my impatience sharp as a serpent's tooth, and Isaac usually in festive good humor, we put together his narrative dreams.

Alma finally accepted nine o'clock in practice but once a month asked me, with a slight smile, what was wrong with me this week. "Listen to me," she said, wagging a finger, "stop eating chocolate cake. You'll get rid of all your crazy thoughts about being sick. Look at me. I swim."

My health aside, good fortune in the sort of class Singer and I conducted fell on us with the occasional appearance of a class character. Someone drunk would do, or stoned or talky or dumb. Not throwing up or violent, they could be messengers of union as well as disruption, and I did not reject them on principle or pedagogic practice.

In 1986 our class character helped take the collective mind off the inanities of the class's important writer and the other teacher, who weekly worked to take his private mind away from symptoms of dizziness. I don't know whether the class character was really dangerous or not: students periodically warned me that he said he'd like to bring a rifle to class and kill us all. Once he spoke about a bomb. He was admitted to the class because he wrote well enough to be there; the Singer show encouraged him to blossom in his eccentricities.

A fairly slight youth, he had dyed blond hair and rode a bicycle and was forever being stopped by policemen for being in places where he shouldn't have been. I doubt that Singer, in his withdrawal, knew of the young man's existence, even though he interrupted me with non sequiturs as often as Singer himself did.

Once the student came to my office and said he'd like to be friends and asked me to go to dinner with him. "I always take people to dinner that I hate," he said.

I said, "I pass."

I saw him on one occasion chewing up a piece of paper. I asked him what he was doing, and he said, "Getting ready to spit this at you."

His stories were about misunderstandings where he was proven correct but given brief jail terms. He was frequently, he said, mistaken for a homosexual in his short stories. Sometimes he was just incoherent. He looked up in surprise as he read one story, and said, "Everyone gets taken for being a homosexual." When no one spoke, he looked at me, and asked, "Don't you?"

I said, "No."

"I do all the time," he said.

Another time, relevant to nothing at all going on, he said, "I once stole a pair of panties from a woman I didn't like and cut them into pieces with a scissors."

He turned in a short story in which God was the narrator. I'd had such stories before. Marked by deep seriousness, or delighted with their ribald humor, students watch the teacher's response to what they consider wildly imaginative and provocative fiction. It is a grand moment: top this, creative writing class.

He had a half smile as he read the story, and Singer said little. With lines accustomed, I asked the student why God hadn't learned punctuation better and why the arbiter of all perfection in this universe hadn't accomplished more in His spelling. "I think this story reads as if it were written by someone pretending to be God," I said. "I don't believe your main character is plausible at all. He never learned to spell, and someone who controls the solar system surely has access to a dictionary."

I asked him later in class, "Why do you talk when you have nothing to say?"

He said, "It gets dull in here. I try to liven it up."

With the class wondering what he was going to do next—and many of them liking him for his zaniness—Singer and I were able to lose ourselves somewhat in the antics of a God-sent class character.

Thinking about Singer Mondays virtually made me dizzy with glucose descent. I asked my friend Kathleen Gordon to come to class for certain sessions. I knew Singer wouldn't approve of working with a woman—if he noticed—but I couldn't grant him the courtesy of his wishes from a prone position on the floor while the class wondered why I'd swooned. Kathy knew my situation. While occasionally I felt a glucose fuzziness at the hopelessness of our performance, the worst never happened. Kathy came—a great favorite of many of the students whom she'd taught in a lower-level class—and departed without adventure.

The misapprehensions about Isaac Singer at the university, some never to be clarified, centered not only on the man in the classroom. An older student, seeing Singer strolling with me on campus, conceived the idea that he had a worthwhile project for himself and Isaac.

"Will you arrange it," he asked, "to have Mr. Singer work with me on a thesis in Yiddish. I think I can get the English departments's okay."

I had known the man years earlier when I had arranged for him to take classes at no cost in consideration of his senior status.

"Mr. Singer's eyes aren't too good," I said.

The man looked at me in amazement. "It's in Yiddish. I'd do it in Yiddish. He'd love doing it."

"Out of the question."

"Why?"

"Mr. Singer doesn't do thesis work."

"Is this your rule or his?"

"The Bible's."

He felt bad at the exchange, a gentle man, and turned at the door to my office. "Say," he offered soberly, "it'll be okay with me if I work with you in Yiddish."

"No, thank you," I said. "I'm not generally available in Yiddish."

Desperate after my semester of swoops and pirouettes with the Singer class, I put on a twenty-four-hour heart monitor in September 1986. For all I knew it might be my heart making me dizzy, but my heart read normal. I no longer needed the dizzying beta-blocker. I was almost happy.

By the time I saw Isaac again in the fall of 1986 he was swinging about more than usual in his moods. He seemed more tired than ever. He occasionally became disconsolate and euphoric—in the space of a half hour. He was having trouble with his vision and hearing, but he kept his health situation from me in detail because he assumed I'd fire him. Nothing I said ever persuaded him that I was not in command of the university. One might be friends with such a person as me, but never trust him with your livelihood. He had little to fear from me; I had been a flack with him for so long that the time was past for redemption by a late honest denunciation. He and I were long-time con men together.

Singer had told the class at our writer's workshops that all publishers and agents were crooks, earning a quick laugh from the group, much in the style of telling *Time* that while some men wanted a harem he wanted a flock of good and reliable translators.

He called me when he read the *Time* article to reassure me that he hadn't meant me; and I warned him that his present publishers and agent would not care to hear themselves so described. He told me—I'd been there and so had my colleague, Peter Townsend, and more than twenty other people—that he'd never said such a thing. I assured him that if he knew not to make these loose condemnations again no harm was done.

A week later he told me in his most forceful manner that he was searching—through his secretary—for a new publisher and a new agent. I advised him to be wary. His agent was just fine; his publishers were people of good reputation. No, he said, they promoted other writers before him. He did not have good financial agreements with them. He had heard that Saul Bellow had gone to another publisher and been given a million dollars. "Could this be true?" he asked me, and I said, "Isaac, it could be true, but it shouldn't mean anything to you. What if I worried about someone making more money than me?" It was a point not even to be discussed by him: his silence stated eloquently that I did not deserve to make more money.

I knew something about the syndrome Singer labored under. There is a quality about men and women who work to create drama in fiction that essentially forces them to inject drama into their lives. They run away from families. They denounce organizations they've loved. They reject agents, publishers, their own subject matter, cities, critics who have befriended them; they change styles and hair-dos. Don't other people too? Not as noisily, craftily, or with as much style.

A friend of mine in Miami, a man of sound sense and an Emmy, perhaps two, wrote a book in six weeks that was made into a movie that overall, he told me, earned him $700,000. When I asked about it in New York, the impression there was that the sum was accurate. Coming back from New York that summer, I told him about a fine time I'd had with my agent, two of her other clients, and a young woman editor. We'd gone down to the Village and had eaten in an Italian restaurant, drunk wine, and talked until late and in little groups walked to our places, still talking, up Fifth Avenue. My friend said, "I never did that with my agent" and the next week called my agent, who must have assumed he'd gone mad. He had an excellent agent, had become rich with her, and was on the prowl to improve his fortune—because, I believe, he wanted to be taken in a friendly band to dinner in the Village on a summer night.

Listening to Isaac, I heard the voice of drama unplayed, dissatisfaction endlessly renewed, calling. He continued to cast about hoping that in one great decision he would rectify a lifetime of perceived wrongs and create a reversal of fortune, like a character in Greek theater. He had no original assailants: only agent, publisher, wife, reviewers. He complained bitterly about his life as a writer.

Sundays, when we prepared to adjourn, I went into the drugstore on the corner of Isaac Singer Boulevard and Harding, and he usually cheerfully said, "The New York Times, you can't be without it." I said either, "I must know this week's greatest writer of the century," or, "Maybe I'll find out the truth this week." Sometimes he waited for me till I came out and I told him what was reviewed on the front page of the Book Review.

These angry mornings, he said unhappily, "Why do you waste your money?"

He condemned on these days everything connected to New York publishing. Names of people I had thought were friends of his were dismissed with a wave of his hand. One critic, he said, "put words into my mouth. I never had such a conversation with him in my life."

In a reckless mood, like the one surrounding The Penitent, he now said, "You see, I was right. The book did very well." He seemed genuinely pleased about something connected to the novel.

When he shouted, "This is Isaac Singer!" on the telephone, was I hearing an assertion there? A challenge? He seemed again bold, fueled by his uncertainty.

We were working one day in Surfside when Singer began to laugh very hard. His face turned red. He stopped talking until he could compose himself.

"I'll give you an idea for a story," he said. "A good mystery story."

I waited patiently.

"To tell you the truth," he said, "I don't know the story, but I know there is a man missing and people are walking around his apartment looking for him. The mystery is this: Where's the cat?"

"I guess whoever took the man away or if the man went away himself—they took the cat too, or he took the cat," I said.

"My dear man, how do you know there was a cat?"

"Well, you said that was the mystery."

"Maybe there was no cat."

"So there's no mystery."

He began to laugh again, until his eyes watered.

"Did you ever hear of such a story?" he asked. "Someone asks, 'Where's the cat?' The missing cat will help solve the mystery, but no one knows if there was a cat there."

"What made them ask?"

"It was a place there should have been a cat."

"Where do you think the cat was?"

He leaned toward me and took my arm. "Who knows if there even was a cat there? Who knows?" He went over the matter in his mind. "Call the story, 'Where's the Cat?' "

"Okay."

"This is a funny story to you?" he asked.

"The cat drowned in the toilet bowl," I said. "I knew the cat."

"See," he said, laughing again, "you have an answer for everything."

He and I gave up Danny's that day for the Singapore Hotel a few blocks away on the beach. Again sharp and unhappy, Singer sat with me there and alluded to Bellow's million dollars. He resented my affection for Bellow's work.

"Why shouldn't you like him?" he asked. "You're both from the same place."

"He's from Chicago, Isaac," I said. "I'm from Pittsburgh."

"Same thing," he said.

Once, at his apartment in New York, I found a copy of *Him With His Foot in His Mouth* and asked Isaac if I might borrow it. He said, "No."

"You're not going to read this in a million years," I said. "What's the sense in keeping it around here?"

He reluctantly agreed to let me have it. "Tell me, what kind of title is that?" he asked. "What kind of writer is he?"

I tried to explain the story "The Silver Dish" in the collection. He listened and said, "Phagh!" as if tasting bad medicine.

" 'The Silver Dish' was in *The New Yorker*," I said, and he became downcast, but he did not condemn Bellow any more that day.

In December we sat on a bench across from the Bal Harbour Shops. He was in a flip and irreverent mood. In the restaurant, where Alma had joined us, he had said of a certain man, "He is a pig."

Looking puzzled, Alma asked, "Isaac, why do you call that man a pig, you don't even know him?"

Singer said, "I know him and he is a pig, and, you, my dear woman, are also a pig."

I laughed, and said, "That leaves only you and me, Isaac. What are we?"

He thought for a minute, and said, "Pigs too. Do you think I'd leave you and me out when I was naming all the pigs in the universe?"

On the bench I did an imitation of a drunken neighbor of mine on Robert Street, where I was born, singing in the morning, after a long night, "Moonlight Becomes You." Isaac was delighted and asked me to sing again in the man's sappy crooning voice.

"You must call your next book 'Robert Street,' a book about your youth," he said.

I said, "You call your book *In My Father's Court*, one of the great titles of the century, and you tell me to call my book 'Robert Street.' You didn't call your book 'Krochmalnal Street.' "

He nodded as if I hadn't spoken.

" 'Robert Street,' it's a wonderful title," he said. "You see, it came spontaneously, that's always the best. When you think of a title instantly it's the right title. Intuitive is always the best for a writer."

He pointed to a woman across the street heavily made up, perhaps late sixties, with four-inch heels and in a dashing white tunic with a

golden necklace. "You see her," he said, "she's looking for romance
and all that she has in life is a new diet. One day God will make
everybody thin and no one will have anything to talk about."

"She looks like she's about to run a race," I said. "Anxious."

He laughed. "You know what she'll tell you? She'll tell you she's
growing."

Before our semester began, in January, he called me with excitement in his voice and said, "I must speak to you."

At breakfast at the Singapore, he said, "We will move together to
an apartment and we will work together. We will help each other out.
I'll help you and you'll help me."

"Where will all this take place?"

"Miami Beach."

He was not joking.

"Where will money come from to support my family?" I asked,
knowing where matters generally fell apart with him.

"I will pay you."

"Then it's not a partnership; I'd be working for you."

"No, we'd be partners. We'd work on each other's writing."

"But how will I pay *you* if it's a true partnership?"

"I don't want any money. I want us to live together and work."

"Now, truthfully, Isaac, how would you help me with my writing?
I know what I'd do with your work, what we always do, but what will
you do for me except pay me? I'd be working for you is what it amounts
to. Full time."

"I'd give you advice. I'd give you titles, ideas."

He brought up his vision of a two-man writer's colony again, then
again, in the following weeks. I told him finally what I made at the
university, not magnificent by the world's reckoning but enough to
discourage a genius's mad dreams of a slave with a sound command
of American idiom laboring over unpublishable, yellowed-at-the-
edges manuscripts and miraculously—he believed in divine will—
making art of them.

"I will pay you," he said, quietly, slipping into vagueness at the
mention of a specific sum.

"And the benefits, medical care, insurance, tuition remission for my youngest—he wants to go to law school."

"We must make it work out." He said, "We will write many books together," and sat back sadly.

We were in the green-and-bamboo lobby of the Singapore Hotel; around us red-faced tourists looked about for adventure, knee-soxed in bermudas, showing their age in folds at their knees, happy and bright on their winter vacations. Isaac, melancholy and small, sat back on the rattan furniture. His desperate distraction from old age had ended for the moment. He said no more that day or ever again about the two of us escaping on a raft down the Mississippi, a venerable Huck from Warsaw and his faithful Jim.

PART THREE

Recognitions at Midnight

~ Chapter Seven

I HEARD A disturbing tale from my chairman about Singer. Bowen told me that a football player had been told by the director of composition, Ron Newman, to straighten out his absences with his instructor, Leonard Singer. The football player mistakenly called *Isaac* Singer at home and then, according to Bowen, called Newman to tell him that he liked Mr. Singer very much. Mr. Singer had told him he was only at the university once a week and it would be fine if the football player should stop by then. He also told the football player that an angel had spoken to him in a dream and told him a stranger was going to call and offer to help him rewrite all his work. But, said Isaac Singer, he was going to resist the offer, and he bade the football player goodbye.

It was in this atmosphere of angels and summations of his career that Singer told me one morning the time had come for the two of us finally to write a great book together. The book was to probe the depths of what he truly believed, he said, not the lies he had told in his autobiographies or the pretenses he had fed interviewers over the years. His genuine philosophies would be revealed, his feelings about Jews and gentiles and America, candid, no holding back. It would be a work that would change people's minds about him. He had regretted falling into untruth; now, before it was too late, he and I would correct the misimpressions. He wanted at first, he told me, simply to go through his autobiographical works with me and correct every misstatement he'd made. Now he felt the two of us would write together a master work, and—the economic climate in publishing encouraging him—said we would become wealthy together on the book.

"We can make a million, yes?" he asked at breakfast. There was a slight tremble of anticipation in his hand for the work ahead of us.

"Two," I said, "one for each of us."

"My friend, this book means so much to me I'd give you all the profits. It must be written."

I was skeptical and abrupt. "Let's talk about it next week," I said, wondering what fancy would strike him over the next seven days. He had said he wanted to write a screenplay with me too, about a month earlier. But this was more serious to him. He called me every day for a week about this important, last work.

I stalled. Alma, too, knew about the great work, which removed it from the momentary smoke of Isaac's fevers. She had never before been involved with Isaac's dreams of writing something final and complete with me. On the following Sunday, I told him frankly that I thought he'd soon break off the writing on the great book and sensibly return to what he did best. Our short story world was, as always, good, vivid—no sign there of the intruding angels in his dreams.

"No," he said, "this is my true life we'll write together."

"I don't want to work on a book like *The Penitent*," I said.

"No, no, this will be a great book. I will tell every detail of myself I have left out. No one knows about me."

He had talked to me ever since I'd known him about lies he told about himself. Modern, I thought first it might be about sexual aspects of himself. But these he had discussed with me—and others—as readily as one talked about rain.

My theory ran at this time, as I watched Singer delight in bamboozling me and anyone else who took him for his Puckish persona, that Singer was himself deceived. He eventually never told himself the truth about what he loved, how much money he had, what convictions he held. *Shtetl* habits of stealth—perhaps a matter of individual psychology in Isaac's case, after all—kept him prudish, intact, reclusive, and split. He was a petty swindler, charming in his belief that no one knew, keeping it—I say it in charity—from himself and then, terrible vision, from his God. Singer buries $140 in a mattress, turns his eyes heavenward, and tells that God, with Whom he is as deceptive as he is with himself, "I'm a poor man, Lord, I haven't got a nickel. You know there's no $140 in that mattress."

As a new semester began, the deadly attributes of our class could have defeated the Royal Air Force and Churchill in World War II. They didn't need the team of Singer and Goran to test their remorseless ineffectuality. There were too many people enrolled. We had thirty. About half of them were Communications majors, from a writing teacher's point of view a condition akin to original sin. Only prayer and four years of classes in literature could redeem them. Communications majors may be interested in writing, but it is screenplay writing. An epithet among Communications majors is that something is "linear"—that is, it doesn't tell its story in pictures or movement or, among subterraneans, special effects. "No one *writes* special effects as we understand the term in English," I say to them, but I don't know whether they're listening. They hadn't enrolled to study with Isaac Bashevis Singer. Requiring a second major to graduate, many of them elect to take a creative writing track in English. Some do quite well as soon as they understand they're not doing something that's a poor substitute for a screenplay or a photograph. They are bright and concerned with the world. Others, requiring a 500-level course—that's Isaac and me—take the course as they would any course, in which they have to pinch themselves to stay awake. They have mostly never heard of Singer.

There were also several self-appreciating graduate students in our last full semester, as well as that other nonmystical element (teachers will say it's magic why some classes are good and others the nadir of all that's rotten with the human race): unmannerliness. They were as a group unnecessarily argumentative, playing to each other for laughs or outrage.

One youth, of otherwise ordinary bearing, poked his head up after some weeks, looked around the class, and asked after I discussed the order of business, "Do I have to read my story to him?"

I said without smiling, "If that's what he wants."

The young man apologized after skipping two weeks, but the apology was private and it wasn't to Singer. It wouldn't have mattered.

Singer, through inattention or his increasing hearing disability, hadn't heard him.

I was as ponderous as a rock laden with jargon sinking to a bottomless sea. I wallowed in frustration, a combination of resentment, giddiness, and unspent information I had bottled up. In the fall semesters when I taught the same course by myself I burst forth with a tongue of fire in assault-weapon bursts. I gave unsuspecting and startled students three times their money's worth. As spring approached with its paralysis, I began to groom those who wanted to go on with advanced creative writing in the courtesies of dealing with Isaac Singer. Respect his age and position: pay no attention to what's said or going on in the front of the room. Whatever you think, it's a wonderful experience. My iron-clad regard and pretense of belief in his classroom wisdom was so reassuring in front of classes in public performance that I seldom heard complaints about him. Only the most direct of our students spoke to me about his inattention and deviousness and they were outraged. Sitting in our classes, most students told me it seemed as though they were watching an interesting comic argument between old friends, a valuable and entertaining exchange. For himself, I'm sure Singer wished on more than one occasion that I'd never had my brains muddled by an American education. I belonged with my people stealing corn from chickens as my mother had once done in Bialystok.

I asked a student, one of my best, David Hart, a Canadian by background, what he liked best about the class, and he said, "It was comical."

"Singer said funny things?"

"He did funny things. When you talked he'd be dozing or looking out the window and then he'd suddenly interrupt you. He interrupts everybody."

"Were you laughing at me then? Sort of old windy being cut off?"

"No, him. He was just comical. He paid no attention to anything and just talked when he wanted to. He was funny when he interrupted everybody."

"Was there anything he said that was valuable?"

"Not too much."

By 1987 Isaac's infirmities were the norm mostly. His disabilities directed our Flying Dutchman as surely as did rude students, the large number of students generally, and the disrespect that many of them had for the writing process. They were students with too comfortable a view of their own place in the writing pantheon. I was tired of it all and wondering why in the world Singer didn't give it up. In our unhappy number were a few of the good students who managed to be there in any disorderly company. They were uncomfortable, stalwart, and seemed, to my subjective appraisal, numb as Mondays dragged on with a class that had the quality of utter failure about it. A large number of the people in the class were young men. The class felt like a locker room with, "Yay, boys!" and all the field bravado necessary to frighten an opponent's baseball team. They intimidated me; they bored me. I swore that this semester with Singer was the end. In a class without Isaac I could handle them; a hostage to Singer's good reputation, I was forced into reasonableness, the death knell to a teacher's control of a class like this.

After one particularly grueling session, a few visitors came up to Singer to get autographs. He signed patiently as our class left the room. Members of another class came in the door. These Middle Eastern students, many with problems in English, were unfailingly polite, attentive, and eager to please. About five of these young men sat together in the empty classroom talking among themselves as the visitors left. Singer stood to leave too, but he apparently determined on departure to be as popular as the day he was born. All charm, he approached the boys from the next class. "Thank you, ladies," he said to them. "I learned a lot today, believe me. It was an outstanding class."

All of the boys nodded. On leaving, he bowed to them. "Thank you," one of the boys said.

Singer bobbed and bowed once more and left with me for the limo. "Nice," Singer said. "They are good students this time."

• • •

Singer and I worked on the gems that became part of *The Death of Methuselah,* laughing at our whimsies, outwitting the world outside the game room together, and plotted a great book.

When Singer asked me in 1987 to find him a new publisher who would give him a huge sum for our masterpiece—he told me the morning of March 15 that his secretary had "fired" his publisher and agent—I thought of Gordon Weel.

"She didn't fire me too, did she?" I asked.

"Not me either," Singer said, and laughed. He was as contented as I'd ever seen him. I suppose he enjoyed having the dirty work done elsewhere: he could shrug and say, "She did it."

"Does she have another publisher and agent?"

"Yes, she has another agent," he said and told me her name.

"Good agent," I said. "But there was nothing wrong with Bob Lesher."

"I'm not going to tell him."

"Isaac, he's going to know. You're impossible."

"I'll keep them both."

"Christ, Isaac, you're going to meet yourself coming and going."

He leaned forward. "He still has things of mine," Singer said. "You see?"

"I see you're nuts, Isaac."

"So, why should I be different?"

Gordon Weel, in semiretirement in Miami, had for twenty-seven years been a sales manager for three prominent publishers in New York. He knew people in publishing who were to me figures in history books. When I asked him to help Singer—who wanted his new agent to come into the deal only after Weel had explored the territory—Weel agreed. He tried over the next few months to sell the great work. As he jockeyed for the sum to approximate what Singer had read that everyone but he was earning, the project turned into three books Isaac was offering and God knows what else. Chopped and diced into the *tzimmis* (stew) Isaac concocted old manuscripts hidden in his New

York apartment. My own sense was that Isaac might be either punishing his publishers for what he saw as their neglect of him or jockeying for a better deal or, probably more likely, looking for signs from them of greater love for him. But later in March Singer signed and sent a letter, at their request, to a publisher who seemed to want the book Weel offered. Other publishers were attracted too, exchanging correspondence and calls with Weel, but I dragged my feet in being specific with Gordon about my working on the project.

I finally told Weel to call it all off as far as I was concerned. I did not know what Isaac wanted. His million dollars—of which I was to get up to 90 percent, depending on his mood (sometimes we were to do it for nothing, give it away, just to see the truth in print finally)— would have to wait for the arrival of the Messiah. He asked me to get my lawyer son, Bill, a young man looming large in Isaac's hourly imagination of impending legal tragedies awaiting him, to draw up a contract between the two of us in which he bound himself somehow to me as literary collaborator for eternity.

"I'll give you 90 percent of what we make," he said, bringing back again with poignancy my poor mother Taibele Silverman and her imaginary fortune she would give me.

"I want 110 percent," I said.

"Please, don't joke!"

"Isaac, for me, this is not a money-making relationship between us."

"What do you want?"

"To leave my son in peace. I'm not signing any agreements with you. You have a publisher. You have an agent. You have two agents. Let's be friends!"

"But we will work together?"

"Forever," I said, "forever and ever."

There is a concept among Jews called *edelkeit*. It is a condition of scholarship, love of God, humility, kindness, and gentleness that serves as a model for what decent, pious, good Jews should aspire to in a world that's unkind to them. The banished Irving Howe speaks of it in Singer in *World of Our Fathers* and notes that Singer is famous for his perversely finding the quality not in the commonly accepted rabbinical or learned professions of service to the human race but in lowly folk, strange outcasts and misfits in the eyes of society. I conjectured when I read the recently detested Howe, after the descriptions of myself by Singer as "normal" and "noble" and "natural aristocrat like your mother," whether Singer had mistakenly placed on me the burden of being a good person, one wrapped in *edelkeit*. We were both literary men: Gerasim, the peasant who carried the dying Ivan Ilytch on his shoulders, occurred to me as a Singer ideal of our relationship. Perhaps Singer, who loved the story, thought of Tolstoy and Gerasim. But my occasional image was more out of Evelyn Waugh's A *Handful of Dust*, where at the end of the book the traveler is taken prisoner by a literary fanatic, an ancient reader of Dickens, and kept in a deserted wilderness a prisoner, reading to the old man until he himself perishes.

Later in the spring, Singer called me one night and said, "I'm in trouble. You must call your son for me. I am going to jail."

Alma seized the phone and shouted, "He's upset. He's crazy."

Isaac said, "Leave me alone, I'm going to jail."

"Will you tell me your alleged crime?"

"Income tax! They want money from me, they say they will put me in jail."

Alma, pulling the phone from him, said, "It's a simple matter. It's nothing. It's nothing."

Isaac said, "Call your son."

"Isaac, listen, if it turns into anything, I promise I'll call Bill. But you'll see, it's nothing. No one is going to put an eighty-year-old Nobel Prize winner in jail for nonpayment of taxes. I promise I'll call if anything is wrong with you and the law."

"Your son will help me?"

"I'll call him at three in the morning if it's serious."

"You will?"

"I promise, any time of night or day."

"Ah, I feel better."

"I'll go to jail for you, okay? That's how sure I am it's a routine thing."
He brightened. "We will go to jail together," he said, his voice light.
"We will do much writing in jail."

I laughed, and said, "I didn't say I'd go to jail *with* you. I said I'd go
myself. Going to jail is a way of getting away from you."

He laughed too. "But we will work together?" he asked.

"You'll send me the manuscripts from prison."

"It's not a joke," he said before he hung up.

I never heard a word about the matter again.

In class a short story was turned in that had its origins in the Mad
Max movie creations. The story, written by a male, was about an arid
desert land that had no gasoline to run its automobiles—a teenage
boy's vision of hell. The sexes had their private interests in 1987.
Sooner would a male in class write about abortion than would a
female write about her out-of-gas automobile in a deserted, barren
landscape of the future. For male Communications majors, the deso-
late future is a genre, and I read to the class some remarks of Otto
Frederick's on theories about the popularity of end-of-the-world
visions and Isaac was pleased. That I read from a book to verify my
thoughts was a marvel to him. The story was bloody awful, and the
student was in a paroxysm of inverse correlation of appreciation for
himself directly proportional to the worthlessness of the story. Singer
hadn't followed it and the class didn't like it, so the student sulked,
the class had red meat to disfigure, hating it with passion, and
another week passed.

The following Sunday Isaac called in what had now become his
customary frightened tone. "Lester," he said, "the story this week is
plagiarized. I think all their stories are plagiarized. We are being
deceived."

"Which story?"

I hadn't known when I was well off. Isaac Singer reading student
stories was a hazard greater than Isaac winging it. After the Oudens
caper he had made stabs at understanding what he was talking about.
After ten years of dodging he was discovering plagiarism.

"I forget which story."

"They're mostly lousy," I reassured him. "Who would write or print such stories anywhere you could have seen them before?"

"I know in my heart this story is plagiarized."

"Give me a hint and I'll look it up."

"We are being deceived."

I had left him in Surfside three hours earlier, and he had seemed fine at our "translating."

"It's a serious charge," I said. "What do you want me to do about it?"

"Make the student confess."

"We have two student stories. Which one is plagiarized?"

"Both," he said. "I have a feeling somehow all the stories this year are plagiarized. Wait, Alma wants to talk to you."

Alma came on and said, "Listen, Lester, he knows what he's talking about. He has seen these stories. He doesn't make mistakes like this."

He called me again Sunday night and asked me what I planned to do about students' plagiarism, and the next day, Monday once more, I became so dizzy in my morning class I had to come home to pull myself together before he arrived. By the time the Singer class started at one fifteen, I felt better, and he never mentioned plagiarism again.

Reading Singer's story "The Interview" to the class that day—he always interrupted to say, "Slow, slower," when I read anything, particularly of his—I shouted each word, pronouncing it with a diction like a rendering of the old "March of Time" newsreels.

Predictably, as he did to students, he shouted at me, "Louder, please, louder, don't mumble." The angry boys in class applauded in derision of both of us, and Isaac, hearing the applause, looked about smiling. When I resumed, he shouted, "Slower, please, slower."

I put my hand up for quiet. "Isaac, they are laughing because I'm shouting and reading as slow as a human being can."

"Go on, please," he said, losing himself in his story as I read.

On March 23 we hit the lowest point in a class that had descended, I thought, as far as American higher education could go. That day—

the one in which the young man had demanded to know if he must read to Singer—the student story was by Joan Miller, a graduate student who earned an M.A. in English that year with a creative thesis, a short novel. She used the word "impotent" in her story and Isaac was enraged from that point on. He sputtered about the word, lecturing her about such language. But, if there was a moment when I knew the game was up with us, it occurred in the middle of Joan's reading her story.

"Louder, please!" Isaac said.

She tried, for her, shouting.

"Listen," he said, beaming and pleased, "you read like this: hauf-hauf-hauf." He imitated a dog barking loudly.

Joan turned to look fixedly at him. She is a quiet person, but who knows? I suspected what could happen would put us in the morning papers. Should I cancel the class immediately by shouting "Fire!"? Composed, she continued to read.

"Hauf-hauf-hauf!" he barked again, louder.

She read again, pausing while he barked at several points. I apologized to her when she went to her seat and said, "Well, you are Miss Congeniality this term." She was shaken, but friendly. She shrugged, and I said, "Thanks."

On the walk to the limousine, I was furious but said nothing. He stopped and took my arm. "You college professors don't tell the truth," he said, "but I tell the truth. Today, I told them."

"What did you tell them?"

"I told them they bark like dogs. They don't know how to read. I told them, yes?"

We slogged through the rest of April with disorders and retreats on our great book and other diversions in his hectic attempt to start life anew.

In class, in one story there was a husband, a wife, and their pilot flying over Africa. Singer insisted that the wife and pilot were in love with each other, although the story was about curious sites in Africa with little concern for any of the three characters. A second story, before Singer flew the coop two weeks early, was slow to glacial in movement, so Isaac said, "What was his name? The story is influenced by that man, what's his name?"

Familiar with Isaac's repertory of contemporary evils, I said, "Pinter."

"Pinter?"

"Yes, Pinter."

"Yes, Pinter. Is that his name?"

The student said she'd never read Pinter, and Isaac said the story was copied from something of Pinter's. I said something monumentally unmemorable to get to three o'clock and the sun quietly set on us as a team in the worst class of our decade together. I went to Bowen after class and I said, "The Singer class is over, with me anyhow."

He said, "It's up to you, but I think we can work something out."

"I'm done, Zack, I'm done, I'm done."

The situation with writing our illusionary masterpiece, now called *God's Fugitives,* was one in which the autobiographical book's prewritten drama would obviously far surpass anything we could write. Of the other, untranslated novels, Alma had, in a conference at Danny's with Weel and me, told us that these novels were in danger of being stolen. She wanted me to have the books. The idea that his secretary would seize them scared her. The idea that I would have them (to hide?) caused my glucose to soar. Alma was supposed to bring them down to Miami in April. They were described as falling apart with age, and I was to have them duplicated.

But it rained in New York when she was packing to bring the old manuscripts, Alma said, and she couldn't find an umbrella. The books still languished in New York, as fragile a hostage to fate as the Singer silverware.

Later, when Isaac was in New York, he called me and told me to fly up to get these manuscripts (he did not offer to pay). It was a plane I knew foredoomed to crash about Vero Beach, so I wanted little to do with those books (whatever they were, he said the manuscripts ran to fifteen hundred pages). There the matter stood as his abbreviated semester ended: Isaac enthralled with his coming fortune on his next to last day in Miami until fall, Alma fluttering about us with plans for the hidden manuscripts (and making plans with Weel to have a moving company pick the books up in New York to elude enemies while Weel was to search for funds to have the books translated so that Isaac and I could put them into English). I told all parties I would have the books duplicated, but there my role as guardian would irrevocably stop. I would enter a monastery once the books were duplicated.

I joined Singer for breakfast on Friday, April 17, since he was leaving the next day. He spoke grandly as we ate of our great, wealthy days ahead. In the middle of breakfast—he had been studying me with a piercing glazed look—he said, "We will write the book now, this minute. We will begin *God's Fugitives* now!"

"I don't have a pencil," I said. I picked up a napkin. "This is the only paper I have."

"Now," he said, "here's a pencil!"

He seized a fork from the table and thrust it at me.

"Isaac, this is a fork," I said. "I can't write with a fork."

"Ah, I'm losing my mind. Here!"

He picked up a butter knife and put it into my hand. "Write," he said. "Write on the napkin!"

"Listen," I said, "give me back the fork. I can write better with a fork anyhow."

He asked, "You don't have a pencil?"

"No, I have a fork."

"A fork? Wait, I'll get a pencil."

"No," I said, rising, "let me take care of it."

I felt that in his state he was capable of bringing back to the table an egg salad on rye and asking me to begin his memoirs with it. From one of the waitresses I took a small pencil and Singer began to write his life, the oft-told tale (it appears in Buchan's 1968 biography) of how he was actually born in a certain village different than the one with which he has been identified. I wrote until the nub of the pencil was quickly exhausted. Nothing on that napkin or what he told me as I nodded in appreciation hadn't been related numerous times.

"I see you like it," he said. "I can tell."

I nodded. I nodded again.

"Well," he said after a while, standing, "we made a good start today, my friend, this will be a book, huh?" He paused to drink the last of the half-and-half on the table and said, "We will make much money together, you and I."

I wasn't sure that Isaac, who was addicted to defining himself, could ever stop. I recognized *God's Fugitives* was the last gasp of the impossible; but was I watching a great writer flailing about to retain his identity or was the spectacle one of Isaac Singer creating a funeral pyre to leap on when this book, as it inevitably would, failed to be written? I had given him over the years a sense of renewal, of redefining himself and striking new stances, of comfortably relaxing in old ones, of perhaps discovering things about himself as he put together his answers to me. He had come to a time with me, apparently, where the end of my role as interviewer was in sight. There would be no further ironic poses, no memories brought to life for both of us.

As we walked that day before he left for New York, he asked, "Wait, did I tell you about a brothel?"

I said, "I'm not sure."

"The first time I ever went to a whorehouse," he said, "I was a very young man. It was two women there and, I don't remember, I was with someone else and he waited for me. The prostitute turned around, you know, and put her behind up to me. I didn't know what to do. I wrote my name on her backside."

"What did you write?"

"My name: Isaac Singer."

Deedee asked me that week, "Why are you doing this, Les?"

"I think it's the right thing."

"You know if by some miracle he could do another book it would have nothing to do with you."

"You mean he's twisting me again?"

"You know it."

As certain as the comets blazing out beyond the solar system, in Isaac's mind was that the great joy in this project would be leaving another confederate at the dock as his ship sailed for a new land. Wrapped in his burning desire to come clean once and for all were the warm, sweet moments when he could cast off everything that was not himself and be resolutely free.

The best of Isaac Singer would endorse my late messianic streak in helping him, use it, even sneer at its perversity, but admire the unworldly foolishness of a middle-aged lad from Bialystok. I had told him—to silence—how my mother warmed frozen food in her cold hands in the old country and stole the food for chickens for herself. The worst in him would enjoy one more trick (I did not take it personally). He'd lead me up to the bridal canopy and then unceremoniously turn and run out of the synagogue—not do the book at all, stop halfway through, do it, hide it, claim he was a sick old man, and survive!

I was on the side of his survival. What did another thirty days of daydreaming with Isaac Singer amount to in a good life without him thus far?

I had nine novels of my own, a loving family, and I acted in the Isaac Bashevis Singer drama, too. My graduate thesis at Pitt was on the fraudulent artist in the work of Henry James, and I felt close to James, to the essence of fakery in Singer.

I had, that spring of academic nightmares, been talking over lunch, as I had for decades, with my colleague and friend, Gene Clasby, about some of the scenes of my youth spent growing up in an Irish Catholic neighborhood in Pittsburgh. Clasby had the disadvantage of actually being Irish Catholic himself and being born among Boston Catholics; thus, I could enlighten him weekly on what it was to be really Irish—at least, what it was to be joyously Jewish among them. One day he was particularly insistent that I begin putting these stories I told him to paper, and the result was that over a two-year period I wrote two collections of short stories and a novel set around a drinking club called The Irish Club. All that summer of 1987 after

Isaac's departure and my reprieve from stewardship—I prayed—I worked on my own things.

In July, Alma came on the phone first. "Wait," she said, "Isaac wants to speak to you."

He said in his most anguished voice, "I am not a traitor to you. I would never betray you."

"I don't think so for a minute."

"We will work together, yes?"

"We'll see."

"Do you know no one knows how much God has meant to me," he said. "We will write a book about what I have never told anyone, how much God means to me."

"I'll look forward to it."

"We will make much money together," he said. "But don't ever forget this: I am not a traitor to you."

"Good night."

He called two weeks later and said, "You are cold to me. You think I have betrayed you."

I will never know the specifics of my betrayal or whether Isaac spoke in his cosmic generic voice. The penny-ante scams on miniscule sums of money, the early annual retreats from our class, the make-a-million book he thought he tempted me with, or the great revelations I would share with him all suggested themselves to me. Or maybe he had mocked my Minsk father, an orphan, a fortune teller, a junk man who drank too much, or my mother and regretted it.

My betrayal of him was worse. When I knew that he had little to say that would help our students in their writing (three sessions of the first course were more than enough to form the judgment), I should have cut it short. When he pleaded with me—at the beginning—to tell him if he was adequate in the classroom, I should have said no.

I never said to him, "Forgive me, Isaac, I betrayed you."

In August, after a long session with Zack Bowen, we decided that the only possible way Isaac, as he slipped into further eccentricity, could be retained at the university was to cut his time in class down to five or six sessions. We would maintain his salary, and that might be all that would be necessary to persuade him. In fewer sessions I could present him as a visiting celebrity—a role he and the classes could relish—and in the other weeks I would myself go over student fiction. We would let his appearances be question-and-answer sessions. I suggest an aphorism for *The Chronicle of Higher Education*: barking at students in imitation of their reading is too much theater for academic freedom to sustain.

When he arrived in September for his annual brief stay in Surfside, he gave me a large manuscript of a novel that he said had been rejected by his publishers and apparently his agent. It was incoherent. He repeated himself every thirty pages. It physically looked like something he had written when he lived on Coney Island in the 1930s. "Here, my friend," he said, "read it, fix it up, tell me what to do."

I did not read the work for three months. Once a week he asked about it, calling from New York. When I called him in Surfside to tell him it was unsalvageable I found him in a jocular mood. Something pleasant was happening in his condo on the other end of the phone. I heard voices.

"Is there anything good there?" he asked.

"Maybe the first twenty-five pages," I said.

"Well, so I wrote twenty-five good pages," he said, laughing. "Good-bye, be well."

Later in September a woman named Shaloma Shawmutt-Lessner asked if I would arrange to have a filmed interview session between Singer and me. She offered each of us five thousand dollars. I agreed but said that Singer's part in the film would have to be worked out between her and Singer; I was out of the Singer business. He told her yes; he told her no. He told me maybe; he told me yes and no in one day. I told Shaloma that her film would be a series of evasions and even hostile answers, but she persisted and he agreed. Still I was uneasy. When I had told him his time at school was being cut to five or six sessions, he had not asked about money, but instead, "Who wants this?"

I said, "Me, just me. Only me. I can't go on like this with the two of us—we're arguing like children in class."

His next question was "What about the limousine?"

And here I failed as a diplomat. Zack had come to my office the week before and asked, "Do you know what Singer's limo is costing us?"

"Yes."

"Twenty-six hundred a semester."

"Well, it'll be less now that he's coming less."

"Can't he take a cab?"

"He can, but he won't like it."

"He can get a cab—we'll pay—or we'll get a grad student to drive him. We'll give the student fifty dollars to do it. *Twenty-six hundred dollars.* How can we justify that?"

I said to Singer, "I think I can keep the limousine coming for you this next semester but it'll probably be other transportation in future years. If things work out with this new system."

"What? What?"

I had never seen him look at me with such anger. I might have been a cabdriver for all that I saw of my old friend in his flushed cheeks and with spittle at the corners of his mouth.

"Maybe a student," I said.

"No students."

"Well, a cab, we'll see."

He paid no attention to me when I said the money would stay the same. The limo was all.

As friends, we seldom talked after that day. I was now on the side of the enemy who put Nobel Prize winners into Yellow Cabs.

In the first day of shooting the film, a student in a mock classroom situation asked him, "What do you think of Professor Goran's work?"

"I don't know him very well," he said. "I haven't read much of his."

En route to a house where some of the filming was to take place, the limousine driver Shaloma had hired became lost, and, as we sat at a gas station while the driver frantically sought directions, Isaac swore he'd never ride with me anywhere. "You have done this on purpose," he said. "You've lost us. This man driving is a murderer, he is calling terrorists. You have brought me to this. I will never speak to you after today."

"Isaac, this is our same limo driver, the young man. Be patient."

Singer was surly at the filming, but there was a pleasure for me in it the first day. Alma wasn't there. But she came the next day, and Shaloma and I argued all day. Alma walked in front of the cameras to tell Isaac to speak louder. Shaloma, who was once in the Israeli Air Force and suffered shrapnel wounds, had never directed a long film before. The waiting between questions and answers was extended. Singer was enraged. Shaloma assured me this was the way films were shot. At the condo where Singer lived we did more shooting, and he became infatuated with a woman friend of Shaloma's on the sidelines. She distracted him. Generally lost, he searched for her outside the range of the lights. He questioned me about her reputation and marital status.

Out on the beach for a final scene, one of the cameramen said, "We can't film here. When he stands against you, he looks like a cigarette that dropped out of your pocket." At the restaurant where we filmed, a cameraman, whose wife was with him, said to me, "We're working on a novel together. Where can we get ahold of you or Mr. Singer when we're through?"

In four days it was over. Isaac said little in the film I hadn't heard before. That Sunday I did not have breakfast with him.

I came to pick him up in January 1988 at the usual place I met him. At the fountain, sitting on a stone bench with him, the wind occasionally blowing spray on us, students sometimes stopped to talk to us. It was not my worst memory, being there. What surrounded getting there was the affliction. After we met, we usually went upstairs into the Ashe Building for our class together. It was adjacent to the fountain, but my January intersession workshop, for which he volunteered with enthusiasm every year, was across the campus. The limousine was to drop him at the customary place at the fountain and then I'd take him to the workshop in my car across the campus.

As I drove up, he stood in the roadway near the fountain blocking my car, frantically waving his arms like a windmill.

"Isaac, it's Lester," I said. "What are you doing?"

"Who?"

"Lester. Are you stopping cars, Isaac?"

"Lester? I never want to come here again. That man threw me out on the street."

"What man?"

He could not explain, but I knew he meant the limousine driver. He sat in my car, and I said, "For God's sake, I meet you here all the time, Isaac. I saw the limo when I came in the gate. You couldn't have been here more than two minutes."

"He threw me out and said, 'Sit there.' " He paused. "Do you have a check for me today?"

In class he rambled and caused the students to fall into an uneasy silence. He terrified me as I took him back to the meeting place and the limo that waited for him. He sat himself in the back seat, and said to me, "Where am I going?"

I said, "To your happy home. Where do you want to go?"

"We don't have a class today?"

"You're coming from class."

He leaned back in the seat and closed his eyes.

In our first regular class of the new semester later in January, he said, "We are not here to talk about me. We are here to discuss your stories."

There was a hushed silence.

I said, "The student stories haven't come in yet, Professor, so if you don't mind, we'll ask you a few questions."

"I'm not here to answer questions."

"It's going to be a long two and a half hours, Isaac," I said.

Singer said, "If Shakespeare were here, who'd want to ask him questions? Don't write like me, that's all I can tell you. If Tolstoy were here I'd rather read his book than talk to him."

I recognized the line from an interview. "But, of course, we're not paying Tolstoy," I said, "and we are paying you."

I went around the conference room asking who each of the students would like to talk to if they were present: Twain, Chekhov (my choice), Thoreau, Dostoyevski, Lawrence. The students had not known what to expect. Less than a half hour had passed. Singer was rocking quietly with a ferocity he could hardly contain.

A student asked a question about whether Singer read any other Jewish writers. He said nothing, and I asked him, "Do you mind if I answer?" When he still said nothing I spoke about the differences between Isaac and more commercial Jewish writers. I spoke slowly: the day was the last one on earth anyhow.

Before I was through, as I paused to catch my breath, Singer pointed his finger across his chest at me and said, without looking at me, "This man doesn't speak for me."

"Well then, you speak for yourself."

Still, he sat silent. Then, without preamble, at the word "university" I used in some context, Singer said, "University! That's what's wrong. They have too many answers and too many professors. The answer to every question should be, 'I don't know.' "

"I'll buy that," I said.

" 'I don't know,' that's all there is!"

"I think students want more from us than that for their fifteen thousand a year."

After class he resumed his cordial manner. He spoke softly, quietly to students. I led him to the limousine, and he was sober. I shook hands with him.

He called that night. He spoke breathlessly. "Alma is signing all my checks. She's stealing. What am I going to do? There's an Arab terrorist in the apartment." Of the last, I understood. It was a young woman with frizzy hair who worked with Shaloma.

"She's not an Arab terrorist," I said. "I know her." About Alma stealing his checks, I told him he was surely mistaken.

I called him later that week because we were supposed to meet on Sunday, but when I told him that the limo would pick him up on Monday at 12:15, he said, "What's 12:15?"

I canceled out for Sunday.

The next week in class, however, he was quite himself. He said he enjoyed talking about himself to students. Ask any questions you'd like. Even in his awful state of decline, catch-up was still available to him. I could not bring myself to walk to the limo with him after class. (The student who walked with him said that he'd asked her, "What is this place?") His sweet performance had shaken me as badly as his bad-mannered one the week before. There was nothing of him left except impulses and fits, moods and contradictory reactions. I felt that his walk to the limousine that day was possibly his last as a Distinguished Visiting Professor.

He was not scheduled, as we had worked it out, to appear again until late February, but by then Alma had broken or dislocated her hip and was hospitalized. He told Shaloma that he thought Alma had run away with another man. He did not call me about coming back to school, and when I called he was so distraught I could not make him understand who I was.

On the seventh of February, Isaac called me at home and said, "Don't fire me. Without this job I'm nothing. People will see I'm just a schlemiel. A limousine comes, I get in on Mondays people know I'm somebody, a person who works. Don't make me a schlemiel, don't throw me into the gutter."

"Please, Isaac, it's not up to me. It's your health. When you feel better, now that Alma's home—let's just give it a rest."

"Where's my contract?"

"I don't have a contract either. They're not out yet."

"But you'll get a contract and I won't. I assure you they don't do this to Saul Bellow. You are throwing me out in the street."

"Isaac, you know I do what I can for you. I'll work for your best."

"I don't know. Can you get me tenure?"

"No, you're not in the kind of job where people get tenure."

"So? You have it."

"I've been here twenty-eight years."

"Is my time there nothing?"

"No, you know it's appreciated."

"People here in the building look at me and they know I'm nothing. On Monday a car used to come, now you've made me nothing."

Alma called in a strained, hurried voice. "You must keep him on," she said. "Please, are we friends?"

"Alma, he can't do it. It's not up to me. We'll try for these few appearances."

"You must keep him on."

"We'll see how he feels."

"I cannot be here with him all the time. You must take him on Mondays."

"We'll see."

"Would you let someone do this to your father?"

When I called Isaac on the twenty-seventh, he was signing autographs in a special edition of one of his books. He had eight thousand books to autograph. "My name is a curse," he said. "I am cursed. I hate the sight of my name."

He called the next day, and asked, "Am I fired?" and I told him he was not. He said, "I've lost my passport. Can you help me get a passport?"

"I guess so. What do you need with a passport?"

"I want to go to France to hide. There's something wrong here. There are people here I don't know. There's women and men, I don't know them. Come and get me."

On March 7, Alma called me from their condominium and said, "Isaac doesn't expect to go back—he knows he's not himself. Lester, it's terrible to see. What a fine mind he had—you know him—that fine mind. You told me something on Harding Avenue that I didn't understand. Now I understand. You said things don't get better when you're old. I had no experience. I was naive. I never saw my mother and father old. They were taken by the Nazis." I thought I heard her crying, but she quickly recovered. "Now I know what you were talking about."

I had told her about my aged parents: my father's descent and then even further falling-away until the end was merciful. When I had told her about my father on Harding a few weeks ago, his situation once like Isaac's now, she asked, "How long did it go on?"

"With him a year."

She put her hands to her face in the middle of the street. "It can go on a year?" I said nothing, and she said, "Longer, it can go on forever. That's what you're telling me."

⁓ Chapter Eight

SINGER HAD A conviction that there was something of himself, a solitary Jamesian "great, good place" where lay truths about himself that only he knew. He had not shared it with anyone. It was as real to him as I was. He defended it with protective moats of good humor and a self-deprecating quick wit. Before audiences he hid it with adroit dissimulations. His secrets lay like an old hidden garden. Its existence was probably never known by his brother, certainly not Alma. He intended at that late date of conspiracies and programs finally to take a stranger down its secluded paths. I had no sense the revelations were of sordid or nasty business. These were not the usual dreads hidden away for fear of blackmail or disgrace. These were complements to half-revealed "truths," explanations. They were to be what he felt, truly felt, not ironical thrusts from the fencing figure who turned aside genuine specificities of emotion or intention. It was, as I heard it discussed and watched it change, variously about details of his life, his feelings about women, the horror of existence, his relations with the Almighty (not like Twain's, filled with rancor, but, as he tried to reveal it to me, more congenial than anyone dreamed—but perhaps this was Plan D, a defense put together hastily as other strategies of concealment failed him). He was sure the time had come. He was eighty-three, and he had waited a long time.

For my part it would have been dim-witted of me not to recognize that there might have been sham to Singer's burning desire to involve me in a truthful book about his life—a net cast out to keep captive the person he believed caused the tinted-windowed limousine to arrive regularly on Mondays. I do not think so, or that it was mostly so; something ate at him, obviously ran in his work, that was different than the transparent huckster who dealt so lightly with unconditional truth. I believe, like others near their end, that he wanted—if not in a will—to make a final announcement about himself. If it tied me to him, so much the better: the statement in its unambiguous clarity was all. For my part, trailing along in his ardor for summation, I was not entirely sincere. I did not think there would be such a book for apparent reasons.

There was manipulation perhaps, from Singer, but only at his usual edges. My crime was worse: I doubted the aesthetic of his great moment of truth, its philosophical resonance, his psychological depth about himself, and practical considerations in his dream of a last word. I did not think him well enough physically, either. He was sound enough for our leaps into the illuminations of his short story world, but he could not physically endure the work of a long book.

Lastly, he was bound to the conditions of his publishing contracts, and children along Sixth Avenue knew that publishers have option agreements in their contracts with writers on future work. It was a book he wanted to be separate from the rest of his work, and that was impossible.

There were, it strikes me now, three reasons why Singer sincerely and fervently prepared to assault the secret repository of hidden truths about himself and could not eventually reveal anything to me. First, it is possible that the habits of seclusiveness he had acquired over a lifetime could not be broken. He could not expose himself to anyone—to whatever degree—after holding on to this vision of a shining city. When he tried, if he did, nothing came but things he was bound psychically never to reveal, and he consciously buried it once more. Then again, perhaps it was me: perhaps he decided to retain his secrets, the truth about himself, for a future auditor he could trust more. Dealing with me, our resentments and arguments passing before him, rather than our affection, he held back at the last minute.

But something else happened as I watched Isaac trying to tell a final truth about himself. Willing with all his heart to use me as the instrument for revealing these secrets—still trusting me until it was painful to him to be so bound to someone else, eager and anxious—he reached into what he thought was hidden and discovered nothing there. And he shrank from the spectacle of his golden city ruined and finally empty. Not that there hadn't been plenty there once; but he had, through all of his thousands of interviews, short stories, essays, and novels, already told it all in one form or another. Dissipated or elaborated, written large and beautifully, all that he was had been laid bare in his work. The secrets he held were only nagging suspicions that something else remained to be said. Now the time of the peak of his powers had passed, and even what he thought hadn't been said was gone, too, never to be recovered.

On September 4, a fiery hot day, I went down to Surfside, and he lay still on the couch while Alma and I sat in chairs and Alma told me a report about a woman we both knew who had apparently had a heart attack in a hotel lobby in Haifa. Isaac lay flat and immobile. He wore white socks and his tie was fastened securely at his collar. He wore his seersucker suit and underneath the jacket was a pale sweater. It was hot in the condo, too.

He said, lying still, unmoving, "Why don't you two stop gossiping?"

Alma said, "Isaac, it's Lester."

"I know who it is," he said, only his lips in motion. She and I spoke for a few more awkward minutes and Isaac sat up and, not looking at either of us, said, "I'm sick of this gossip. Can't you talk about anything?"

Alma said desperately, "It's Lester, Isaac."

He lay back on the couch, rigid, as white as his socks.

I stood and said, "I'll go now."

"Isaac," Alma said, "Lester is leaving now."

He said nothing.

"I'll go to the elevator with you," Alma said, her shuffle pronounced. "Isaac, I'm going down to the elevator with Lester."

Outside in the corridor, I said, "I can't come back."

"Come for me," Alma said, "you're doing it for me."

"No, Isaac hates me. You know it."

"He doesn't know what he hates. One minute it's one thing, another time it's another. Don't take what he does so seriously."

"Alma, I can't ignore it. He's going to say something terrible to me."

"So?" she asked. "It won't be him speaking."

"It will be me listening."

At the elevator, she stepped on with me. I pressed the hold button. "Listen," she said, "don't abandon me. I have nobody. Call me."

"He'll be angry," I said. "You call me."

"You and Deedee mustn't abandon me."

"Can't you call me? I'll come whenever you need me and I'll do whatever I can to help you, but I can't come on my own. He's ready to explode at me."

She waved her hands in the air and said, "I don't understand you. You take him seriously. You know Isaac."

"You'll call me and I'll come, I promise," I said as she shuffled off down the corridor.

A week later my dean and chairman drove up to Surfside to have lunch with Alma and Isaac. They'd both wanted to retain him as long as his health allowed, all three of us agreeing that a proper gesture would be that he continue to receive his salary, even if he made no appearances at all on campus that semester, even the one after that. Isaac and Alma quarreled all through the lunch, Zack said, and interrupted each other. For the longest time Zack thought Isaac's railing against the person who had brought him to Miami and then abruptly humiliated him by firing him was directed at the president of the university. "Three quarters of the way through lunch," Zack said to me, "I realized Singer was talking about you.

"I tried to explain to him, 'Lester hasn't the power to fire you,' but he wouldn't hear it. I asked him if he'd come back to teach when he felt better, and he said, 'Yes, but without Goran. I won't work with him. He says peculiar things in class and nobody knows what he's talking about and I have to keep explaining to the students what he's saying.'"

Isaac Singer in his first open-to-the-public appearance on the campus of the University of Miami in February 1979, a night festive and welcoming with people standing in the aisles of the six-hundred-seat theater, and yet the poignancy of the battered hat and the bent old literary warrior and the distance between even hat and man speak of Singer's essential and remorseless loneliness.

Perhaps Zack Bowen was pulling my leg.

The lunch went fairly well; but Singer afterward refused to ride in the car with the men when they brought their car around to the restaurant to drive him home. He chose to walk—I'm sure, not trusting either of them or anyone else out of the terrors that lay on every side now. (Weel had once taken him to an Internal Revenue Office. He had refused to leave the car.)

Alma did not call me, but I called again, on September 30, as I had at the end of all the months Isaac and I had worked together. I hoped to talk to her, but Isaac answered the phone. After considerable confusion, he understood who I was.

"What do you want?" he asked.

"I want to bring your check down to you in Surfside. Like I always do. Maybe we'll have breakfast."

"Why do I need you to come here? Put the check in the mail. Who needs to see your face around here?"

"Shall I have them put all your correspondence in the mail too? You don't want me to be in touch with you at all?"

"Of course. Who wants you around here?"

"Goodbye," I said.

He hung up without saying goodbye. The last time I was to see him was the day when he lay so white and otherworldly and fully dressed on a hot afternoon in his white socks on his couch.

Reading in the *Times* one day after class that the fly-by explorations of Jupiter had shown that there were twenty-three lightning flashes a second on the giant planet, Singer turned from the newspaper to me, and asked, "What do you suppose the Almighty had in mind out there?"

He loved the extraordinary planet. The universe endlessly confirmed his panic and his wonder about it. He remains for me the spokesman of our dilemma of unbelonging.

~ PART FOUR
# A Clear December Day

⌇ Chapter Nine

W HEN I THINK of him at our best, it is a sunny Friday with the passing
of the old year in the air and the phone rings, a last call from Isaac
Singer before 1987 ends. He is making groaning sounds and he asks
me if I could "rescue him." I am alarmed at his voice. "What is it?" I
ask, and he tells me he has fallen and injured his thumb and it is
turning black. It is a clear day and I am having an old friend over for
dinner and my thoughts are not with Singer. "Please come, help me,"
he says. "I have no one."

December 30. I do not think he and I can go on any further as
teachers, but it is Isaac Singer, a victim of the planets and history,
and I can't deny him. "I'll ask Deedee if she can come," I say.

At the mention of her name he brightens and asks to speak to her.
She comes away from the phone tense and expectant. "He seems to
have really hurt himself," she says. "He wants us to take him to the
hospital."

"Where's Alma?"

"He wants us."

Our ride on a beautiful Miami morning is awkward. Isaac calls me
at the time of hurricanes offshore to tell us he fears his television is
going to explode. He phones to ask shyly about his checks, hoping to
trap me into confessing that I have concealed one from him. He has,
in the past, phoned me to come and take him to my doctor in Kendall,
an hour from Surfside. I call a friend of mine from Pittsburgh living
in Surfside, Billy Gorin, and he finds Singer an excellent physician
within minutes on Isaac Singer Boulevard. There will be a call from
him one day, I fear, and it will place us in the final drama of his strange
life. It is his last drama and it will have no illumination in it. Deedee
and I do not speak on the ride north to Surfside.

He is waiting outside in the driveway of the Surfside Towers with a sheepish and confused grin. He shows me his bruised thumb and I don't know what to make of it. It seems to be merely a sore thumb. Seeing Deedee, he says, "Ah, Deedee, come look at it."

She studies it and says, "It's nothing, Isaac, you don't have to go to the hospital with that."

He is as relieved as if a team of specialists from Johns Hopkins has given him a reprieve from death.

"I knew you'd take care of it," he says fervently to my wife. Alma is subdued but smiles happily at Deedee.

The second time Isaac saw Deedee he seized her hand and kissed it and said, "You are as beautiful as a European woman." She is a full head taller than he is and he respects her for her American authority about things. She has medical resources and information never known in Poland. I have spent fifteen minutes getting him to pronounce her maiden name, McDowell. He has, groping for words, described us once as "normal people."

The time of terror passed, Isaac's manner is that now he is with such friends as were never known before in an unlucky life. "Come," he says, "let us go to breakfast."

"It's lunchtime," I say.

"Let's go to lunch," he says. "We'll eat like pigs."

The day has become a good-natured romp. Alma is pleased that what was descending into another day of darkness has brightened into a sunny day. Isaac holds Deedee's elbow as she enters our car. Alma and he sit in the back, and when they are not smiling quietly to themselves I see in the rearview mirror that they are both content.

"This is a beautiful car," Alma says. "What a beautiful car, Lester."

"I bought it last week," I say.

"Such a car," she says. "It's a pleasure to ride in it."

"Lester is a sultan," Isaac says, a familiar word for me in my grand material habits.

"How did you hurt your thumb?" I ask.

"I was running to answer the telephone and I fell on the bed and tripped and fell on my thumb."

"You know, Isaac, you are going to kill yourself one day," I say, "rushing to seize an opportunity. Who the hell do you think is calling you that's important enough to kill yourself for?"

"Well, who knows?"

"I tell him all the time," Alma says.

They are both dressed as for an outing, Alma with flair in a brightly colored blouse, Isaac in his fine, clean-pressed cord suit. I wonder for a moment if we were lured here to wander with them—but, no, his anguish was real. The recovery was a spontaneous Singer miracle of the sort that lifts his short stories and, by the hour, his life.

We talk and laugh in the car in our last hours of friendship. We eat in a Miami Beach restaurant, pancakes and raspberries. Isaac says, "See how a day that starts one way can go in another direction?"

When we're through, complimenting my car continuously, Alma asks me to drive to North Miami Beach to a shoe repair shop. It is a hundred and twenty blocks away. She expresses gratitude with each mile. We are saving her, she says, bus rides and transfers, hours in the heat. The car is comfortable and Isaac sits back in it, studying Deedee through eyes half opened. Once, he says, "This is a happy day after all." I enjoy him back there, and Alma. They love us and are using us and are happy and the moment is filled with friendship.

We are a week away from when I will tell him that we must cut down his hours, three weeks from the last time he and I will ever sit again in a classroom together and institutionalize our failed wizardry, a month away from Alma's fall and Isaac's final dissolution. A good moment. Alma and Deedee go into the shop and Isaac and I sit in the car and the day's shadows are sharp on the street. The sun is beyond brightness in the sky over our heads.

Isaac says when we are alone, "I never should have been born."

"I thought you said back in the restaurant you were happy," I say.

"You have made me happy," he says. "That's why I say I should never have been born."

I watch him in the rearview mirror. His eyes are closed and he might have been sleeping.

"You're such a boy," he says. "Twelve."

We played in our question-and-answer arena a game where each spoke of what was an ideal age for us. He always said—sometimes in a classroom, as we performed—"thirty-seven." This would make the year 1941. He was six years in the United States, impossible to imagine what dreams ignited his work, what women, what books he conceived or was working on. I say, in our game, "seventeen." It was a time of my first freedom, hitchhiking to Atlantic City and seeing the ocean, able to do a turn on fate that had me born in a third-floor apartment on Robert Street. When Singer was angry with me sometimes, he said, "You're not seventeen, inside, Lester, you're twelve! You never grew up."

But today he means something else. He means I am as innocent as a boy in his imagination now as he sits with me in the car, the air conditioning defeating the day, both of us safe for the moment.

He sighs gently in the back seat, eyes closed.

Perhaps he regrets again what thoughts or deeds uncomfortable to him had caused him to say he was not a traitor, that he had not betrayed me.

"I'm happy you were born," I say.

Isaac does not speak further, so overwhelmed is he by his rejoicing in the day and its unexpected pleasures. Life is, after all, not a happy place, he has said in book after book, and in this one afternoon ending an old year things are good. A splendid way to remember him: he and Alma are beaming as I take them back to their condominium—plans for future trips, the car, how grand it will be for all of us to ride, ride forever; and that is how, whatever else lay between us, I want to remember him, locked, for whatever reasons, in friendship with me and I with love for him.

～ Afterword

After Singer died in July 1991, I took a solitary walk around Surfside, trying to recall the exhilaration, wit, and nonsense that had enlightened our days on these sidewalks.

It was a sunny day of the sort we had enjoyed for a decade. There were patches of bright sunburn on the bare arms of the fair-skinned British tourists, and bobbing women past middle age charged into bakeries. Nothing had changed much after three years, and I went into Danny's, but it was too crowded; I walked up to the ocean and stood observing it for a while.

I ventured down toward 9511 Collins, the Surfside Towers, where Isaac had barred me from ever coming. I walked the circular driveway. Was I hoping Alma would appear at the front door, imperious and befuddled, and, recognizing me, find words to reassure me that whatever there was between us that ate at her was forgotten and unworthy of our affinities and affection?

What am I doing? I asked myself, making a pilgrimage of the sort adolescents take to an empty gymnasium where they had once scored well in a certain basketball game. I had too many old neighborhoods behind me now to find comfort in any one in particular. But I did understand, as I thought about it, why I came on a hot day once again to stroll in Surfside. I hoped to meet Isaac Singer in the driveway, hurrying from his condominium building as if in a panic, dashing somewhere, his brain aflame with scenes and characters and paradox and, seeing me there in the sunshine, incorporating me instantly into his giddy, savage world. He would have discovered that I had done him no harm and would make peace on the spot. I would assure him, "Isaac, you never hurt me in anything important."

His books continue to be published, translated, as if he truly were present somewhere else directing the show. Can one imagine that place of reconciliation where he might be? Raging at his enemies and translators, obtuse reviewers, *schmearers,* phonies, communists, and egomaniacs: it is not a place I would want to be, but what a circus!